The Art and Life Library.

EDITED BY
WALTER SHAW SPARROW.

====

VOLUME ONE.

The British Home of To-day

A BOOK OF MODERN DOMESTIC ARCHITECTURE
AND THE APPLIED ARTS.

(Completely out of Print and at a Premium.)

VOLUME II.

The Gospels in Art

THE LIFE OF CHRIST BY GREAT PAINTERS FROM
FRA ANGELICO TO HOLMAN HUNT.

(Published November, 1904.)

====

OTHER VOLUMES IN ACTIVE PREPARATION.

====

HODDER & STOUGHTON, 27, Paternoster Row, London.

FROM A PHOTOGRAPH BY FRANZ HANFSTAENGL AFTER THE PICTURE IN THE BRUSSELS GALLERY.

MADONNA AND THE CHILD JESUS.

· THE · GOSPELS · IN · ART ·

· THE · LIFE · OF · CHRIST · BY · GREAT · PAINTERS ·
· FROM · FRA · ANGELICO · TO · HOLMAN · HVNT ·
· THE · TEXT · BY · LÉONCE · BÉNÉDITE ·
· HENRY · VAN · DYKE · R · F · HORTON · AND ·
· THE · BISHOP · OF · DERRY & RAPHOE ~ ~

· EDITED · BY · W · SHAW · SPARROW ·

THE · ART & LIFE
LIBRARY

H & S

· 1904 ·

· HODDER & STOVGHTON ·
· 27 · PATERNOSTER · ROW ·
~ LONDON ~

Printed by
Unwin Brothers, Limited,
The Gresham Press,
Woking and London

PREFACE

MANY noble subjects enrich the History of Art, and the noblest among them all — the noblest and the vastest—is the subject of the present book. It has been a source of inspiration to nearly all the greatest painters, and a volume as large as the present one might with ease be published on pictures that represent even a single theme, such as the Good Samaritan or the Prodigal Son. For this reason, and no other, it was necessary to devise a careful plan for the general treatment of the book, so that its scope and character might be kept within specified limits. The aim, then, is to gather within one volume a good and memorable selection of works by noteworthy painters from the days of Fra Angelico to the present time, so as to form a pictorial companion to the Gospel Story, but to exclude those pictures which might provoke controversy and give pain or offence in some religious circles. The art represented not only springs directly from the spirit of the four Gospels, but makes its appeal to all who are in sympathy with the general Christian attitude to the Life and to the Work and Teaching of Jesus Christ.

The subject is thus limited, but it still remains so wide that many artists cannot be illustrated. The greatest men are well represented, but among the lesser lights of the old masters and among the hundreds of living painters whose art has been transfigured by the Gospel Story, only two or three, here and there, have been chosen and illustrated as a type of many. Even so, more than one hundred and ten painters are represented in a characteristic manner ; and the number of pages devoted to their work is greater than has ever yet been given to it in a single volume.

One of the chief aims of THE GOSPELS IN ART is to present a great diversity in the choice of illustrations, so that the history of the Gospels may be represented as completely as possible by the pictures. The volume is, indeed, a pictorial Life of Christ.

In order that the book might do justice to the paintings, special arrangements were made not only with Messrs. T. Agnew & Sons, Messrs. Henry Graves & Co., Messrs. Goupil & Co., Mr. F. B. Daniell, and Messrs. Maggs Brothers, but also with the best photographers in Europe—with Messrs. Braun, Clément and Co., of Paris ; with Messrs. Hanfstaengl, of Munich and London ; with Mr. W. E. Gray, of London ; with the Autotype Company ; with Mr. Frederick Hollyer, and with Messrs. W. A. Mansell & Co., the English Agents for the leading Italian firms, Alinari, Anderson, Brogi, and Naya.

It is a pleasant duty to offer sincere thanks to the living painters and collectors who have so kindly given help, and to Mr. David Veazey, who designed the Title Page and the Cover.

Walter Shaw Sparrow

CONTENTS

Introduction

PHOTOGRAVURE PLATES

MONOCHROME PLATES

MONOCHROME PLATES (CONTINUED)

MADONNA DEL CARDELLINO—THE MADONNA OF THE GOLDFINCH.   FROM A PHOTOGRAPH BY MESSRS. BRAUN, CLÉMENT & CO. AFTER THE PAINTING IN FLORENCE

Raffaello Sanzio (Raphael of Urbino)

1483-1520

The History of Art in its Relation to the Life of Jesus Christ

By Léonce Bénédite, Director of the Luxembourg
Done into English by Wilfrid Sparroy

NE may say that the figure of Jesus, even when we do not consider it from the religious point of view, is the sublimest that the genius of art can depict. That of the Creator cannot be defined; it defies the imagination of artists, so that even the greatest masters are unable to make of it anything save a conventional likeness, a likeness that goes on repeating itself without being ever renewed. On the other hand, no more heart-stirring countenance than that of Jesus can haunt the artist's mind; I do not mean a believer's merely, but even the mind of one whose soul has not been touched by the Christian faith. It realizes the divine type above all, this physiognomy of Jesus; and at the same time it realizes as well the noblest characteristics of humanity, for He who has been called the Son of Man was born of a woman. Moreover, if you compare this association of the human and the divine with that on which was based the conception of heathen theogony, you will see the world of difference which separates the one from the other.

The heathen gods are men who, from Olympus where they reign, control the destiny of mankind, like masters of a privileged and triumphant race. Endowed with all the vices of men, the story of their lives, of one and all, is filled with scandalous intrigues; and if their effigies can offer the higher characteristics of physical beauty, of power, or of grace, it is assuredly not among the gods that we should seek, if we would find in antiquity the plastic expression of that sentiment of the divine as we conceive of it to-day. The only signs of this feeling which we could hope to trace would be more likely to be met with among the counterfeit presentments of the heroes. In the beginning, when the first rudiments of Christian art were being evolved, the Christian idea gave a new meaning to forms of the past, and the heroic figure of Orpheus was not unfit to serve as it did as a type of *The Good Shepherd*. But no sooner had art conceived the likeness of Christ, than she informed it with the noblest qualities of beauty to which the human face and form can attain, whether it be in the order of what the painter David called " beauty made visible," or even more particularly in the order of what may be styled " beauty made articulate." For it is precisely this breathing and eloquent beauty which, in the history of civilisations, may be regarded as a product exclusively Christian. With equal truth it may be said that the vicissitudes through which the figured likeness of Christ has passed correspond exactly with the changes in artistic idealism which have taken place, age after age, among Christian peoples.

The conception according to which Jesus was supposed to have been beautiful only in a spiritual and moral sense, and to have been incarnated by the Father in the shape of man, offering, as it expressly did, a contrast to ugliness, made no appeal whatever to the popular imagination, nor, to be sure, did it have the slightest influence on the plastic arts. The iconic type, besides, was not long in concentrating itself at its ease upon a notion which, however much it might be capable of taking on many a modification in detail, character, and expression, would never again depart from such general traits as had been once fixed. And this type is the noblest likeness of a man, with features clear and regular, framed with long hair to the neck, and with a soft curly beard.

With the Byzantine period, whose dogmatic tyranny pressed heavily upon the whole of Christendom, this type was for a long time noteworthy for a rigid majesty, that had in it something wild or fierce, something *farouche*. On the illuminated vellum of miniatures not less than on the ground-work of gold mosaics, this impassive image follows your gaze with its great eyes, fixed and stern, in which the Eastern Church has set the implacable

Introduction

flash of its traditional fatalism. But no sooner has human thought begun to awaken once more and to stammer out, through art's yet halting and naïve tongue, the first wailing cries of life of which it is aware, than it looks up with an unknown yearning to the face of our Saviour. And it is then that this tenderness assumes an aspect singularly significant; for the piety of the multitude and of those who are called upon to give expression to their feelings, spends itself by an act of special worship on the presence of the Child Jesus and His mother. And thenceforward, from Cimabue to Raphael, the countenance of the divine baby lightens little by little with a smile and kindles successively with feelings that grow more and more conscious of humanity.

Nothing is more touching, as nothing is more captivating, than this worship which the early Tuscans and people of Sienna addressed to the *bambino*, and more especially to His mother. On this peerless type of womanhood, shining in all the splendour of youthful modesty, gentleness, and purity, they lavished a feeling of adoration, mystical and emotional, that found its aptest expression in celestial pictures painted with a brush steeped in love. The story of the Virgin, in its varied episodes, became their darling theme, and there is one, the *Annunciation* among others, on which the most modest as well as the most illustrious have expended the most ingenious tenderness and the most refined penetration. Even at Venice itself, after those first attempts, austere and harsh, which look as if they had been confined in the strait-waistcoat of the German manner, is it not yet at Venice that art creates the most suave types of languishing Madonnas—of Madonnas with short, neat nose, with lips plump and loving, with large eyes ineffably gentle—of Madonnas who hug, in the warm caress of their maternal arms, the curly little *bambino* with the dreamy eyes? With what golden streams of amber light, with what deep and passionate harmonies, with what strains of adoration, does not Bellini enwrap these unforgettable creations?

At Sienna, at Florence, at Venice, no stuff is magnificent enough, no brocade is sufficiently sumptuous, no velvet is bright enough, nor are there enough gold and gems and jewels wherewith to adorn the two-fold object of this ardent adoration.

Art has never regained the rapture, charm, and wonder, the first ingenuous freshness, of these sights and visions, nor will she ever regain them. By and by, in the ruined stable, with its tottering walls and shattered thatch, Mary, in her purple robes, kneels before the little being, frail yet chubby, whom she has just given to the Universe and whose life and whose death will shake, to its inmost depths, the old-established order of things. Old Joseph, lost in thought, is seated in a corner; the ox and the ass, even they are scarcely less thoughtful; are they dreaming, perhaps, of the coming of an age of pity for the down-trodden servants of man? And whilst the star of Bethlehem shines in the heavens, a concert of beautiful, young, heavenly choristers fills the air with supernatural voices toned to the purest melodies and accompanied by crystalline harps and viols of gold.

And then, behold! the most extraordinary caravan, the most astonishing and splendid cavalcade, which has ever been seen to thread its way across the sandy tracks of the East. Here are Kings of fairyland, clad in brocade of blue and scarlet, cased in gold armour and tricked out with precious stones, wearing silk turbans laden with jewels and with high diadems atop; forward they ride on white horses richly caparisoned, while, not less sumptuously arrayed, some black slaves who hold the bridles are followed by a procession of fantastic horsemen. First among these come innumerable lords; they are dressed in cloaks, and their tunics, falling in stiff folds, are enriched with a miraculous design of flowers. For headgear, they wear cloth hoods of purple and gold, muslin turbans, and silk skull-caps, or tall hats made of fur. While some carry a hawk on the wrist, others have a monkey on the shoulder, or yet another, a young leopard slung across his saddle-bow. In this magnificent crowd, stretching to the farthest confines of the horizon, are heralds blowing trumpets, huntsmen holding greyhounds in leash, and pages carrying swords and scent vessels or censors; archers there are, too, and servants driving long strings of jaded camels whose humped spines laden with presents keep swaying from side to side. All this phantasmagoria of the East winds across

THE ANNUNCIATION OF THE BIRTH OF JESUS. REPRODUCED FROM A COPYRIGHT PHOTOGRAPH BY PERMISSION OF MESSRS. BRAUN, CLÉMENT & CO., PARIS

Alfred Bramtot

1852-1894

Introduction

a rocky landscape lined with palms or with bunches of orange and lemon-trees bearing golden fruit, while anon a herd of deer, fleeing, scampers from end to end, and a flock of doves wings its flight across the heavens, pursued by birds of prey. And when at length a halt is called, where should it be but in front of the simple thatched cottage wherein Mary of Nazareth has just fulfilled her divine mission. The illustrious pilgrims dismount from their superb steeds; the ox and the ass look round with eyes big with amazement; and, while the blessed star which has been their guide is beaming with an intenser brightness, the three kingly Maji offer to the little child all their power and all their wealth and glory.

This period of Italian art, which runs from the beginning of the fourteenth century to the end of the fifteenth, may be regarded as the golden age of Christian iconography. We follow it from Giotto the Great, of Florence, and his disciples Giottino, Taddeo and Agnolo Gaddi, Orcagna and Spinello Spinelli, or from the Siennese artists, Duccio, Simone di Martino, and the two Lorenzettis, or, again, from that brilliant master Gentile da Fabriano or from the sweet cloistral figure of Fra Angelico, till we pass on to all the incomparable forerunners of the great artistic movement of the sixteenth century, namely, the Florentines, Masaccio and Lippi, Gozzoli and Verrocchio, Ghirlandaio and Botticelli, and the Umbrians, Piero della Francesca and Perugino; and, throughout the period, the story of the life of Christ covers the walls of the cities and churches, the chapels and cloisters, and even the convent cells, with the freshest and most exquisite efflorescence of paintings delicately tinted. In some there is a genuine and childlike piety and a yearning mysticism, and in others a naturalistic passion commingles with a bookworm curiosity, with a taste for the marvellous added; and all is translated, as if by enchantment, into infinite delights, and that with a vivacious impressionability, a spontaneousness, which has died with the rapture that gave it birth.

And if we turn to the northern countries of Flanders, of Germany, or of France, there too we shall find the same virginity, the same religious artlessness of feeling for that hallowed period of art which precedes the sixteenth century.

But doubtless, in so far as the figures of Christ and of the Virgin are concerned, the kind of outward beauty that flourished in the southern countries is no longer quite the same. It is a beauty rather of expression, wrought out of the deep conviction and the earnest and austere faith that prevailed in countries of mist and cold. Seated on a throne hung with garlands and draperies, or with carpets of bold Oriental designs, and looking ever so tiny in her huge robes with crumpled folds, the Madonna, with the broad and rounded brow, with eyes *à fleur de tête*, and the little mouth so full of earnestness above the narrow chin, presents the holy Child to the adoring worship of mighty grandees or well-to-do merchants, burgomasters, aldermen, or plain citizens, who, clad in black velvet, are kneeling opposite to their wives. This is how the virgins of Van Eyck, Memling, or Hugo van der Goes appear to us. In France we have little virgins, coy and modest, with features more arch and delicate, and shapes more gracefully framed.

But more particularly at this time shall we see, in the life of Jesus, the mournful period of the Passion. And here we shall scarcely ever find other than a Christ of sorrow, with emaciated limbs and body, on whom a mother, in tears, flings herself in the midst of women in deep distress: heartrending and pitiable scenes into which the kindly and simple-minded artists, in their emotion, have thrown all their fervent and impassioned souls. And every painter of Ghent and Bruges, of Cologne or Harlem, of Tournai or of Dijon, will pour out upon these touching or dramatic sights the magic of the first deep, fervid, and pellucid harmonies of oil-painting. But with the new times which open with the Renaissance, everything changes in the minds of men. No longer is art devoted exclusively to the service of religion in order to spread abroad its teaching. It is individualized, it grows curious, with a zest for learning and erudition; it extends the field of its comprehension in the direction of nature and of man, and, harking back to antiquity, recently discovered, resumes in a spirit of dilettantism the worship of the ancient gods.

Introduction

Take the great artistic trinity of the sixteenth century. The sculptor who found at his chisel's end the stupendous and meditative image of Moses was not less successful in stirring the hearts of men with some grief-stricken *Pietà*. But the smooth-faced God of the Day of Judgment looks more like a sort of justiciary god of antiquity, while even the picture of the Holy Family, heroic as it is, carries with it not a spark of the Christian spirit. For the matter of that, Michelangelo is always more closely in touch with the Old Testament than with the Gospel. Raphael, on the other hand, has informed his Virgins with a supreme grace all compact of lofty elegance, of noble simplicity, and of modest dignity; while his Jesus, who reverts to the effeminate type of Perugino, is set off with an added touch of free and natural grandeur and a consciousness of His divine mission, which is already shown with singular eloquence in the eyes so intense, so absorbed, so full of heavenly mystery, of the *Bambino* who, in the arms of the Madonna di San Sisto, blesses the World.

As to Leonardo, who has set on the lips of the Virgin and of Saint John a smile so mysterious, he has, with the clear-sighted intelligence of his exceptional genius, understood Jesus and His surroundings so well that his *Last Supper* has become a typical composition from which it has been scarcely possible to break away again in the modern history of the arts. And that is because he has succeeded in portraying the character of each of the apostles with convincing insight, by the groups which they form among themselves, the place which they occupy respectively, and by their expression and their by-play. But the figure of Christ, scarcely visible, alas! to-day on the fresco worn by time's ill-usage, is it not the noblest and holiest and most august embodiment of the Son of God? Upon the simple words which Jesus sadly utters, behold, what an uproar around the table! Surprised attention, indignant protestations, loud outbursts of feelings of dismay and horror; astonishment and terror on the face of the traitor, who alone is modelled in the shadow: while all the apostles reveal by their emotion and wild gesticulations their humanity and their true natures. The gentle Saint John himself, his hands crossed, swoons grief-stricken like a woman. In the midst of this commotion, the greater glory of Jesus is made manifest by His countenance, so calm in its dignity, at once so simple and so supreme, a countenance which, in this company of peasants and fishermen, has an ineffable pathos; it stands out by virtue of I know not what supernatural aristocracy.

Be it noted, after the great schism that split Christendom, the spirit of the Gospels passed over to the side of the Reformation. In the Catholic dominions of Italy and Flanders, of France and Spain, constituted and controlled by the omnipotent Church, overruled by the absolute power, and manipulated or mishandled, now by the Jesuits and now by the Inquisition, only a religious art of a somewhat official kind could arise, an art kept under watch, full of pomp and decorative show. Thus in Italy and in France we notice an emphatic and learned academism, sometimes of professional and skilful virtuosi, sometimes of practitioners a trifle more reserved, who speak of religion with the fine rhetoric affected by the preachers of a worldly turn of mind. Nevertheless it would be unjust if in France, where the Jansenist spirit had stimulated by its austerity the comprehension of religious matters, we did not call attention both to the gentle and dreamy figure of Le Sueur and also to the grave and lofty personality of Poussin, whose philosophic realism penetrated every whit as deeply into the spirit of the Bible as into the essence of antiquity. Nor must we forget that Frenchman of Flanders, Philippe de Champaigne, whose cloistral severity was not proof against his tender expressiveness of touch.

Next, in Flanders, we come to a realism, or rather a sensual materialism, the picturesque animation of which is all on the surface: witness the athletic and inexpressive Christ of Rubens, who suffers with a purely bodily anguish from the spear-thrusts of the executioners and from the tortures of the Cross, whilst Mary Magdalene, weeping, lets the mass of her golden hair fall over her bare shoulders. Or again, we get the ascetic realism, harsh and dour, of the early Spaniards, which is presently softened with a touch of homely grace by the more kindly brush of Zur-

THE MADONNA DI SAN SISTO. AFTER THE PAINTING IN THE ROYAL GALLERY, DRESDEN, FROM A PHOTOGRAPH BY W. A. MANSELL & CO.

Raffaello Sanzio (Raphael of Urbino)

1483-1520

Introduction

baran, or by Murillo's more supple and more persuasive touch.

In this particular century, if you wish to find the true spirit of the Gospels, you will have to go to a little Protestant country, a democratic republic, in the midst of that valiant race of sailors and merchants of the Low Countries, where, in the dank shadows of sombre alleys along the canals, and through the dense haze of sullen skies, Rembrandt's genius of light and love bursts out in all its radiance. And this time, we meet with Him again, the Jesus of the Gospels, the Christ of the meek and the bairns, of the disowned and of them that mourn; the Christ who delighted in the company of women and little children, who gave a welcome to the beggars and vagabonds, and who died the death of humanity between two thieves. And this Christ born among the people and for the people, no class can claim as its own.

And is this Christ beautiful, taken from a plastic point of view? Impossible to say. Doubtless it lacks the elegance of bodily form which is so marked a trait of the Christs of Italy. But what do we care for that? It responds so touchingly to the notion of such a figure that the imagination can picture that we are at a loss to form any other conception of it. And it is, in history, the supreme representation of the personality of Jesus, combining as it does the double characteristic of the human and the divine. Now, Jesus is man, for He is the brother of all men, of the poor and the outcast, of the wretched, and even of the wicked, not less than of the rich and the mighty, the hypocrites and Pharisees. He is human by virtue of His tenderness and love for men, because He is Himself the blood-tie by the aid of which all men shall one day live together in unity, and because He, suffering and dying as they do, gives His life for them. And He is God by virtue of His birth and His complete goodness, the inner essence of His acts, by virtue of His mission and of that supreme emanation that Rembrandt transforms into pictorial presence by means of the magic of clair-obscure: a radiance pouring forth from His whole person and shedding a mysterious brightness over everything about Him. See, for example, the incomparable picture of the *Pilgrims of Emmaus* at the Louvre. The two pilgrims are seated at table. Jesus, full face, is in the midst of them, His long hair falling over His shoulders; and His eyes see above and beyond all things and all men, and His earnest face shines out with an inexpressible sadness. He breaks the bread, and by this sign the two disciples recognise the Master. And notice with what ingenious and acute intelligence, or rather with what marvellous insight, Rembrandt has succeeded in rendering this miracle sensible to our sight. In the upper chamber, lit up by the divine brightness shining on His brow, the Christ is visible to the two disciples alone; for the servant, who comes in to set a dish on the table, lays it down carelessly, without being conscious of the object that fills the guests with extraordinary emotion.

In order to be the Christ of all men, who came down for the multitude's sake and lived here in the midst of the multitude, the Christ of Rembrandt is far from being impersonal. His life unfolds itself amid surroundings that keep the singular savour of their Asiatic local colour. We know what an inquiring mind, what an eager intelligence was shown by Rembrandt in all things, how he loved to know and to accumulate documentary evidence, filling his portfolios with Italian drawings and prints, hoarding Oriental knick-knacks, scouring the quays where the ships land from the Levant or from the most distant countries, haunting the winding alleys of the ghettos, and penetrating with the old rabbins into the deep and ruddy brown shadows of the synagogues. And thus, in his pictures, the splendour of the East and the leprosy of the slums meet with an indescribable mixture of probability and life.

Let us pass over the eighteenth century: it does not precisely shine by virtue of an outburst of the religious sentiment. But, from the first years of the nineteenth century, a wholly unexpected reaction took place, unexpected because the presages of it were hidden in the midst of the general upheaval occasioned by the French Revolution and the Continental wars. It marked a return to the idea of Christianity, with a vivifying renewal of the enthusiasm to which it had long been a stranger,

Introduction

an idea which in Germany, as in France, was confounded with the idea of nationalism. Now the fact is that in this kindling flash of freedom and imagination which we call Romanticism, the very first act of the people was to turn towards the ethnical origin of their species. And hence the passionate interest shown on all sides for the period of the Middle Ages. In England, as well as in Germany and in France, collections were made of the old popular songs; the old *fabliaux* were published, and people fell to reading once again the tales and novels of days gone by. Indeed, in Germany, the society of the Middle Ages was regarded as the ideal of political and social life, and there the mystic exaltation had reached such a pitch that more than one celebrated poet was converted with *éclat* to Catholicism. And the painters, too, caught this contagious asceticism. The famous Overbeck was converted in his turn, and off he went to Rome. There, with a few friends gathered together in the convent of San Isidoro, he founded that group of mystic and Christian devotees which goes by the name of the Nazarenes. With enthusiasm they studied the frescoes and mosaics of the early Christian epochs, long before the Pre-Raphaelites proclaimed the decadence of art after the death of Raphael. And in France, where German ideas had forced their way under the influence of Madame de Staël, we have evidence of the self-same state of mysticism and religious enthusiasm, but it cannot be said that religious painting was cultivated by them in a religious spirit: it was used only as a pretext for historical form and picturesque effect. Still, in this particular field, it would be impossible to ignore the fact that Eugène Delacroix, the leader, has exalted the original inspiration with a dramatic intensity without a parallel since the days of Tintoretto. None has grasped with greater poignancy the sublime tragedy of Calvary.

But the religious development of the school had taken another turn, manifesting itself for the most part in the direction of the classics. Thus the first signs of this were noticeable in the studio itself of the painter David. Among his pupils, indeed, a few young men of a cultivated turn of mind and an imagination tolerably exalted, called attention to themselves, as much by the eccentricity of their antique apparel and the fashion of their beard, as by the originality of their ideas. The name which they bore among themselves was that of the Primitives. More pre-Raphaelite than the Pre-Raphaelites or even the Nazarenes themselves, the decadence of art, in their opinion, started not later than after Phidias. They had three bedside books: Homer, Ossian, the famous Ossian, and the Bible. Into this little circle, which had some trifling influence on David himself, the spirit of Ingres, the future head of the classical school, had penetrated, even before he arrived in Rome; and though his influence was not very marked, it was yet sufficiently so to leave record of its presence. Ingres, too much concerned with plastic purity, although he painted with imposing greatness many a subject of a purely religious order, does not convey any fresh emotions with these interpretations of his. But among his pupils there was a group of decorators, somewhat neglected but extremely interesting, who constituted themselves, more or less intentionally, into a little mystic society. This is what is styled in France the second school of Lyons, for the principal artists, Orsel, the two brothers Hippolyte and Paul Flandrin, Jannot and Sebastien Cornu were natives of that town, where they had been initiated in their art by a painter named Revoil. The latter, with the assistance of two or three other artists, had previously formed the first school of Lyons, noted in the modern history of French art for contributing to the creation of what is called the *genre historique*. These mystics, who lived in Rome in touch with the German Nazarenes, were not less fond than they of everything that stirred the remembrance of the early Church.

Later, on the eve of the Revolution of 1848, in the midst of the moral excitement caused by the propaganda of Saint Simonism, another and a different sort of exaltation arose, a religious and mystic exaltation, which was imbued through and through with the new prepossessions. The chief representative was Ary Scheffer, formerly an exponent of Romanticism. Impregnated to an extreme degree by German ideas, he translated,

THE PRODIGAL SON.   FROM A PHOTOGRAPH BY THE AUTOTYPE CO., NEW OXFORD ST., LONDON, AFTER A PRINT
ENGRAVING

Albrecht Dürer

1471-1528

Introduction

with a sentimentalism which had a European vogue the contempla-
tions of St. Augustine and St. Monica, the meditations of Jesus
in the garden of Gethsemane, Jesus brought before the people,
&c. This sentimental religiosity was continued with ecstatic
and romantic reverence by a group of painters who devoted
themselves to the exclusive worship of the Virgin: *Virgins
Praying, Virgins in Adoration, Mater Amabilis,* or with special
and manifold homage to the heavenly hosts of Angels, Cherubim,
Thrones, and Dominions, whose duties, hierarchies, love-affairs
and portraits, informed for many a long year the pictorial efforts
signed by Tassaert, Galimard, Vincent Vidal, Jannot, and others.
The latter even attempted a first compromise between the dogmas
of the Church and the new ideas by his picture entitled *Faith and
Science joining Hands at the Foot of the Cross,* whilst Galimard
painted and lithographed *Liberty leaning on Christ.* But, somehow or other, these religious subjects, whenever they had some
reference to the Bible or to the Gospels, scarcely ever broke free
from the customary themes of the old masters, and long practice
had quite exhausted their power of appeal. Accordingly, in
order to breathe new life into this moribund form of art, recourse
was had to archæology and, more especially, to ethnography.
Now the French forces had just invaded Algeria, and Horace
Vernet, who had told with a true soldierly dash the story of their
high military prowess, hit upon the plan of reviving these sacred
subjects and lending them an appearance of greater truth to nature
by transferring them to those very surroundings which, as was
supposed, had been perpetuated from age to age without any
apparent change. The result was a long series of interpretations
of the scenes from the Gospels or the Old Testament, considered
from an Oriental point of view. And the ever-increasing travels
of painters in Egypt, Syria, and Palestine enabled them to take
notes, with their eye on the object. Nor can we forget in England
the travels of Thomas Seddon, the author of that curious picture
in the Tate Gallery, *The Valley of Jehoshaphat;* or Holman Hunt,
the last survivor of the Pre-Raphaelite brethren and the illustrious
painter of *The Light of the World.* But the two most celebrated

forms of this documentary realism are those created by the Hungarian painter Munkacsy, and by the Frenchman, James Tissot. The former of these, in a vast composition somewhat theatrical, but vigorously executed and full of colour and of a certain realistic dash, has striven in his *Christ before Pilate*, and later on in his *Christ on Calvary*, to give the effect of the historic truth, the local colour and the moral nature of the characters; while the latter, James Tissot, who during his stay in London had yielded to the temptation of translating the parables of our Saviour by dressing them up in contemporary costume, as in the *Prodigal Son*, was one day overcome with the irresistible desire of reconstituting the life of Christ from beginning to end. So out he set for Palestine, and gave up ten years of his life to the most patient and untiring labour, to the end that he might find himself, historically and ethnographically, in the closest touch with the conditions not merely of the artistic truth and the verisimilitude of things, but also with those of the exactitude and the truth itself. Indeed, one might almost say of Tissot that he is a disinterested observer, so eager is the artist to be quit of his own personality and his own feelings. He reminds us of nothing so much as of one of those intrepid reporters who follow an army in the fighting line.

Such are the principal features shown by the critical spirit of modern history in its relation to sacred art. As to the ideal conception of the figure and the life of Jesus Christ, the most original, perhaps, comes to us from England with the early Pre-Raphaelites, Ford Madox Brown, whose picture of *Christ Washing St. Peter's Feet*, in the Tate Gallery, with its close realism, with the penetrating brightness that lightens up the scene, and with the distinction and the dignity of the figure of our Lord, is one of the most seductive and comprehensive specimens of this sort of composition; Sir John Everett Millais, whose simplicity is somewhat affected; Rossetti, ardent and impassioned by reversion to his southern and Catholic ancestry; Burne-Jones, of a delicately legendary turn of mind in his *Annunciations* and *Nativities;* and more especially Holman Hunt, with his scenes

Introduction

from the life of Christ and his Gospel parables, all handled with the memory of the landscapes he had traversed set in his mind's eye, and in a light so intense that it seems supernatural. And is it not supernatural, after all, this exceeding brightness emanating from the face of the heavenly King crowned with thorns, who, in the star-lit night, lantern in hand, comes knocking at that little mysterious door, half-hidden in a mass of convolvulus, briar, and meadow-sweet? In France those who are rightly called the Idealists, Puvis de Chavannes, Gustave Moreau, and others, take an interest more especially in translating the parables or in choosing for their subjects scenes from the life of Christ's forerunner, St. John the Baptist, in the midst of the typically Oriental surroundings, wild and voluptuous, in which are placed the unforgettable figures of Herodias and Salome. At the end of the century, however, a singular symbolical evolution must be mentioned, as it has a marked bearing on art in its relation to the times and the influence which the thoughts and prepossessions of the day had upon it.

Now Millet, living constantly in communion with the Old and New Testaments, had grasped the full simplicity and grandeur of the most commonplace events in a peasant's life; and one day he conceived the idea (as may be seen in the *Flight into Egypt*, which Mr. Shaw Sparrow has judiciously chosen for reproduction here) of re-setting the scenes from the life of Christ amid contemporary surroundings, without, however, robbing these of their character of poetic generality. Later on he was followed in this attempt by J. C. Cazin. In those days, in France, we were under the new and lively influence of the Russian literature, with its evangelical and humanitarian Neo-Christianity and its doctrines of social equality; and the outcome of this was a Christian ideal more at one with the word of Christ. Now, Cazin, leaning on Millet and on the great memory of Rembrandt, found at last the long-desired artistic formula. His favourite book being the Old Testament and the Gospels, he infused new life into the stories of Hagar and Judith by turning to intelligent and emotional account the reality of the life about him, with its accompanying and expressive local colour. Thus delving he discovered a sort of artistic vein of idealism, at once poetic and realistic, religious and popular, which was worked for a while and on occasion with a fair measure of success. It was to this impulse, albeit with a technical education formed in a different sphere, that we owe the work of such artists as M. Dagnan-Bouveret and M. Burnand, who are still counted among the authorised representatives of the school of religious painting in France. But the continuation of the attempt made by Cazin was made doubly sure by the German painter, Fritz von Uhde, who treated sundry episodes of Christ's life (*The Nativity, Suffer the Little Children to come unto Me*) with genuine emotion and an intelligent assimilation of the surroundings amidst which He lived. By and by, however, this formula degenerated under the stream of new ideas of an ultra-northern origin. Up till then Jesus had preserved his traditional appearance of a beautiful Semitic type with auburn hair. Then, still regarded as the protector of the humble and the suffering and the little ones, as the bearer of the good news of brotherly love, the Son of Man, casting aside His seamless white garments, borrowed the dress and facial characteristics of the vulgar classes of to-day.

Such, down to this hour of writing, are the most original manifestations which have reference to the artistic interpretation of the life and sayings and personal appearance of Jesus Christ. That the last word has been said is not to be believed. The past, great as it is, will not sum up the future. Each century, each generation will have something more to add on this subject which will ever be for the human race of limitless and immediate reality. For all men who have a faith or merely an ideal will feel the need of expressing this ideal or this faith of theirs, and of embodying their pangs and sorrows, their hopes and their love, by reproducing on canvas the personality of Him who was acquainted with every grief, with every anguish, but who none the less blessed life, teaching us that it should be a fellowship of infinite faith and hope with love and gracious charity.

CALVARY.

REPRODUCED FROM A PHOTOGRAPH BY PERMISSION OF MESSRS. W. A. MANSELL & CO.   AFTER THE PAINTING IN THE LOUVRE, PARIS

Andrea Mantegna

1431-1506

The Childhood of Jesus Christ

By Henry van Dyke, D.D., LL.D.

ALL know that the story of the birth and childhood of Jesus the Christ, told with such wonderful simplicity and purity in the New Testament, has taken deep hold upon the heart and the imagination of the Christian world. No other part of the gospel history has given so many themes to poet and painter. No other narrative in the world has been so often illustrated by so many famous artists. It is easy to see some of the reasons which have made it a favourite subject.

First, there is the religious interest which centres in the entrance of the Divine Saviour into the world. Such an event, for all who believe in the Christian religion, must have a profound significance. It is the sunrise of faith, the beginning of a new spiritual life, the laying of the corner-stone of the kingdom of heaven on earth. Even if the artist himself were not sure of this, did not altogether believe it, he would know that other people believed it ; and by the imagination he could see what a supreme importance was given by the faith of Christendom to the brief and simple story of the Birth at Bethlehem.

Second, there is the human interest which clings to the ever-beautiful relation of motherhood and childhood. The tenderest and most unselfish love is that with which a true mother looks upon her little child; the most perfect innocence and trustful joy are revealed in the deep eyes of the baby who smiles into the face of His mother bending above Him. The paintings of the Child Jesus and the Virgin Mary have drawn into themselves the best thoughts of men concerning the gracious secret of maternity and the unstained bliss of infancy.

Third, there is the poetic and pictorial interest which grows out of the incidents of the story, the strange contrast between the heavenly significance of the birth of Christ and its outward circumstances, the blending of light and shade, joy and sorrow, hope and fear, angelic songs and earthly persecutions. All these varied elements, centring about a single figure, afford a field of illumination and illustration such as art loves. For in the great ages and schools of painting the curious theory that a picture must not have a meaning, but must be essentially nothing more than a striking or pleasing arrangement of lines and combination of colours, has never prevailed. Truth of drawing, symmetry of composition, beauty and harmony of colouring —these are essential, of course, to a good painting. But they are only the means by which the painter expresses himself, his thought, his feeling, without words, to the eyes of other men. Great artists have always chosen subjects for their pictures, and for the most part subjects with associations of poetic or dramatic meaning—subjects which appeal directly to a quickened emotion in those who look thoughtfully and understandingly at the pictures. It would be difficult to say where one could find more of such subjects than in the story of the Child Jesus.

My first advice then, to those who wish thoroughly to appreciate and enjoy the pictures reproduced in the section of this book for which I have been asked to write the introduction, would be to read and re-read the Gospel of St. Matthew from the eighteenth verse of the first chapter to the end of the second chapter, and the first two chapters of St. Luke's Gospel. Then it would be wise to read some of the later legends which were woven in the apocryphal books, and in the mediæval poems and narratives, about the birth and childhood of Christ. Many of these legends are curious and fantastic, evidently allegorical and symbolical. They have none of the simple directness and quiet restraint of the Biblical history. They are, in effect, clear illustrations of that native trait of the human mind—familiar to every one who has tried to tell a true story to a child—the craving for picturesque detail. " How did it happen ? Where did it happen ? Who else was there ? How did they look ? What did they do afterwards ? " These are the questions that children ask when they hear a story; and these are the questions to which men have given fanciful answers in the apocryphal and mediæval legends, such as the *Protevangelium of St. James, the Gospel of St. Thomas, The Gospel of the pseudo-Matthew, The History of the Nativity of Mary, The Golden Legend* of Jacobus de Voragine, the poems of Konrad of Fussesbrunn, Walther of Rheinau, the Abbess Hroswitha, and the traditions given by Justin Martyr, St. Jerome, St. Bernard, and many other writers.

Much of this legendary and symbolist material was taken up quite naïvely by the painters and embodied in their pictures. I do not know precisely what illustrations are to be chosen for this book, and so it is impossible to trace the influence of the legends in detail. But suppose you have a picture of the Annunciation, which represents Mary as passing through a garden when the angel came to her; this is in accordance with the *Protevangelium*, which says that Mary was chosen by lot from among the virgins of Nazareth to spin the royal purple for the Temple-veil; one day, as she was returning from the fountain with her pitcher of water, the angel met her and said, " Hail, thou who art full of grace!" and when she went back to her spinning he came again to her to complete his message. If the picture represents Mary in the house working at the veil, the artist has chosen to show us the second appearance of the angel. The emblems which the artists put into their pictures are significant. The pot of lilies at Mary's side, the lily-branch in the angel's hand symbolize purity. The olive-bough borne by the dove means peace.

Or here is a picture of the Nativity which shows the Child and His mother and Joseph in a cave. This is according to the account of Justin Martyr (and quite in harmony with the customs of Palestine), that the stable of the inn where Christ was born was a grotto in the rocks. Here perhaps you see the ox and the ass bowing their heads before the Child. This is told by the *Gospel of the pseudo-Matthew* in fulfilment of the prophecy of Isaiah, "The ox knoweth his owner and the ass his master's crib." Here, again, is a dazzling supernatural light radiating from the Child, so that the shepherds who have just entered must shade their eyes. This detail is given in many legends.

Or look at some of the paintings of the Visit of the Wise Men. They are three in number; they are dressed as kings; one of them is old, one middle-aged, and one young; often a black man is represented among them. Here we see how the story has been developed from its simple form, in the second chapter of St. Matthew, where nothing is said about the number of the Magi, or their ages, or their royal rank, into the full, rich, symbolical narrative of *The Golden Legend*.

The five chief points around which the paintings of the birth and childhood of Christ naturally group themselves are (1) The Annunciation, (2) The Nativity, (3) The Adoration of the Magi, (4) The Flight into Egypt, (5) The Home at Nazareth.

1. The Annunciation comes from the first chapter of St. Luke, and with it are associated two minor incidents—the visit of Mary to her cousin Elizabeth, and the birth of John the Baptist, the forerunner of Christ. The painters have delighted to show us the virginal beauty and meekness of Mary; the joy with which the angel brought his message, the awe and wonder with which she received the new conception of her son as the Son of the Highest, the Saviour of His people. No picture of the Annunciation is good in which this wonder and this joy are not expressed. If in addition the painter has chosen to put in many details to make us feel the innocence and lowly grace of Mary's life; if he has shown us the quiet work with which she is busy, the sweet order of her room, which images the tranquillity of her soul; this also is well. But the great thing is that he should perceive and show, as simply as possible, the charm of that perfect figure of maidenhood, no rude peasant-girl, but one with royal blood in her veins and heavenly thoughts in her heart.

2. The pictures of the Nativity have a greater variety of incidents and of modes of presentation. The simplest are those which show Mary and Joseph in the stable with the Child; then come those in which the angels appear, or the

MARY AND THE CHILD JESUS.

shepherds came to pay their adoration; another conception represents the Mother alone with her Babe, adoring Him or nursing Him. Pictures of the Presentation in the Temple, and perhaps some of the Madonna and Child, belong to the general theme of the Nativity, because their central idea is the advent of Christ as a little babe.

Here the painters have found a wide field for imagination, and have used large liberty in expressing the feelings with which different persons drew near to the Holy Child. Mary is almost always shown as wondrously happy; sometimes, as in Murillo's "Adoration of the Shepherds," lifting the cloth that covers the Child and displaying Him with gentle pride; sometimes, as in Correggio's lovely little picture at Dresden, bending over Him in a sweet rapture of tenderness which makes her very hands tremble with joy.

All worthy representations of the Nativity in art, however they may differ in minor details, whether the painter has tried to reproduce the scene with faithful realism of costume and surroundings, or has transferred the event to a setting frankly drawn from his own age and land, should have, I think, this one quality in common: they should make the interest of every figure in the picture centre in the Child, and most of all, the mother's interest. They should lift up and glorify maternity and infancy by bringing before us in visible form the conception that the birth of Jesus, to those who realized, however dimly, what it meant, was the dawn of a new day of hope for the world. To do less than this would be to fall short of the first requirement of the realism of the spirit.

3. With the Adoration of the Magi, a new element comes into the scene. These wise men from the East, whether they were kings or not, were the representatives of the outside world. Their homage typified and foreshadowed the worship which was to be given to Christ in coming centuries by the rulers and teachers of the Gentiles.

There are pictures which show the Magi on their journey led by the star, sometimes shining in the form of a babe in the sky; and others which show them at the court of Herod asking their way; and others which show them being warned by an angel in a dream not to go back to Jerusalem; and others which show them returning by sea to their own country. But the great majority of painters have chosen the moment at which the gifts of gold and frankincense and myrrh were presented to the Child. Here there is room for splendid colour and dramatic contrast.

But how did the Child receive the gifts? Was He sleeping quietly? Did He reach out in childish glee to grasp the glittering tribute and play with it? Did He lift His hand in blessing, with a divine intimation of the meaning of the strange scene? Who knows! The evangelist tells us nothing of this; and the artist is free to give us his own interpretation of the prophetic scene.

4. The Flight into Egypt is the contrasting companion-piece to the Adoration of the Magi. The one brings the great world into the dwelling of the Child Jesus; the other carries the Child Jesus out into the great world.

The pictures of this subject fall into two main divisions: those which represent its actual journey, and those which show the Holy Family resting, either by the way or in the land of Egypt. The paintings which deal with the latter theme—commonly known as the Repose—include some of the most beautiful works of art, especially during the last three centuries. Many details have been introduced from the legends of the Flight, in which the apocryphal *History of the Nativity of Mary* is particularly rich. This is one of them: "The Holy Family rested by the road beneath a date-palm, and Mary desired to eat of the fruit; but it hung high above her head. Joseph, being weary, was not able to climb the tree. But the Child Jesus knew His mother's wish, and at His command the tree bent down its branches. Then He thrust His finger into the sand, and a spring of water gushed forth. The next morning Jesus thanked the obedient tree, and promised that one of its branches should be carried by the angels and planted in Paradise." Here

The Childhood of Jesus Christ

is the origin of all those paintings of the Repose which show the Mother and Child beneath a bending palm-tree. Another idea has been introduced by modern painters, who show Mary and the Child resting in Egypt, while above them is seen an image of the goddess "Isis, the good mother, the faithful nurse, suckling her infant son Horus."

With many pictures of the Flight an allusion to the Massacre of the Innocents is naturally joined. Sometimes it is made a companion-picture. Sometimes it appears as a distant scene in the background. But the most beautiful and significant connection between these two incidents has been imagined by Mr. Holman Hunt in his great painting of "The Triumph of the Innocents."

The landscape is half-shadowed by night; but the moonbeams weave a filmy radiance over the plain and the distant hills where the watch-fires are glowing red. In front marches Joseph, with his basket of tools on his back, a sturdy son of toil. The mother, a noble woman of Palestine, carries the Child in her arms, happy and fearless. But who are these little children that run and float beside the travellers? They are the spirits of the murdered innocents of Bethlehem, set free to follow the infant Saviour, and knowing that through Him they have entered by the gate of death into eternal joy. Three tiny ghosts in the rear have not yet felt His presence nor caught sight of Him, and the pain and terror of mortality are heavy upon them. But the others are radiant and rejoicing as ransomed souls; and at their feet rolls the river of life, breaking into shimmering bubbles, in which the glories of heaven are reflected. Joseph does not see the spirits. I doubt whether even Mary sees them clearly. But Jesus recognises His former playmates with joy. He leans from His mother's arm to greet them, holding out a handful of wheat, the symbol of the bread of heaven.

Is it all mystical, visionary, unreal? Or is it a true picture to the eye of what faith beholds in the religion of Jesus? Surely if this gospel has any meaning it is the bringing of light and blessing to the suffering little ones of earth; a deeper compassion and a tenderer care for them; and the promise of a heaven full of happy children.

5. After the return from Egypt comes the home-life at Nazareth, the household joy of the Holy Family, the education of the boy Jesus, the friendship with His little cousin John, the pilgrimage to Jerusalem, and the finding of the young Christ in the Temple among the doctors, hearing them and asking them questions. There were intimations and forshadowings, no doubt, of the high and sacrificial mission that lay before the boy Jesus: there were talks with His mother, who had kept in mind the mysterious events of His infancy and pondered them in her heart. But there were also hours of quiet study over the book, and of lonely, happy wandering among the hills, and of joyous pastime with His playfellows, and of patient labour in the carpenter-shop of Joseph. Does not the record tell us that "Jesus increased in wisdom and stature, and in favour with God and man?" And without study and work and play, without companionship and solitude, without watchful care and wise freedom, such gracious growth from childhood to manhood is impossible.

The artists have given us their visions of the way in which these elements may have entered into the life of Christ. I do not care to ask for a historical proof of every incident that they have chosen to depict. It is enough if they have done their work reverently, with thoughtful imagination, and with the painter's skill which lends a speaking beauty to the picture. It is enough if they help me to feel the divine charm of the boy-hood of Jesus and realize the certainty of the Eternal Wisdom that entrusted the Saviour of the world to the care of such a mother as Mary and such a guardian and protector as Joseph. It is enough if they make me remember more clearly that the Lord and Master of us all grew up in a simple human home, ruled by

"Pure religion, breathing household laws."

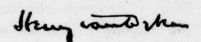

THE CHILDHOOD OF JESUS CHRIST

THE STAR OF BETHLEHEM.

REPRODUCED FROM THE WATER-COLOUR DRAWING IN THE BIRMINGHAM GALLERY BY PERMISSION OF THE FINE ARTS COMMITTEE

Sir Edward Burne-Jones, Bart.
1833-1898

THE CHILDHOOD OF JESUS CHRIST

THE ANNUNCIATION OF THE BIRTH OF JESUS.
REPRODUCED BY PERMISSION FROM A COPYRIGHT
PHOTOGRAPH BY FRED. HOLLYER,
LONDON

Sir Edward Burne-Jones, Bart.

1833-1898

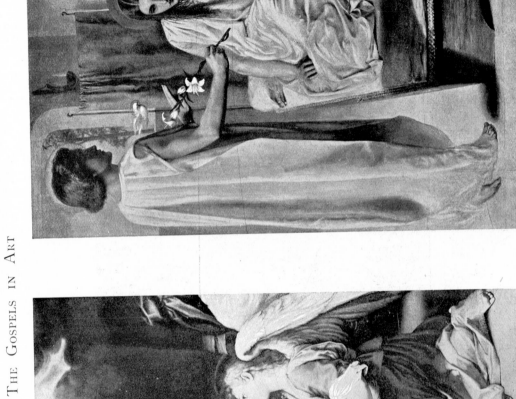

THE ANNUNCIATION : ECCE ANCILLA DOMINI. REPRODUCED
AFTER THE PICTURE IN THE TATE GALLERY, LONDON

Dante Gabriel Rossetti

THE ANNUNCIATION OF THE BIRTH OF JESUS. FROM THE PICTURE IN THE
MUSÉE DU LOUVRE, PARIS. A COPY AFTER FEDERIGO BAROCCI

G. B. vista Salvi (Sassoferrato)

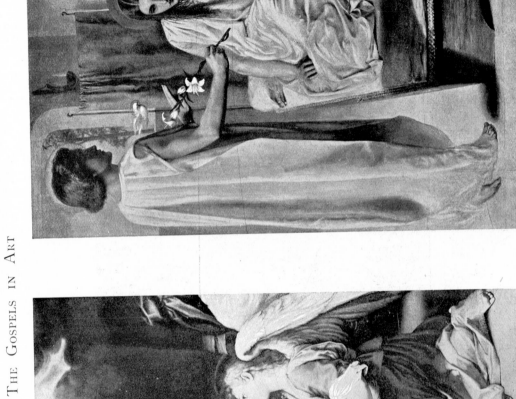

THE GOSPELS IN ART

50

THE VISIT OF MARY TO ELISABETH. AFTER A COPYRIGHT PHOTOGRAPH BY MESSRS. BRAUN, CLÉMENT AND CO., PARIS, FROM THE ORIGINAL DRAWING
IN THE ALBERTINA, VIENNA

Leonardo da Vinci
1452-1519

THE MEETING OF MARY AND ELISABETH.   FROM A PHOTOGRAPH BY MESSRS. W. A. MANSELL AND CO.
AFTER THE PICTURE IN PARIS IN THE MUSÉE DU LOUVRE, No. 1321.

Domenico Ghirlandaio

1449-1494

THE CHILDHOOD OF JESUS CHRIST

THE VISIT OF MARY TO ELISABETH. FROM A PHOTOGRAPH BY ALINARI AFTER
THE FLORENTINE FRESCO IN THE CHIOSTRO DETTO DELLO SCALZO

Andrea del Sarto
1486-1581

THE BIRTH OF JOHN THE BAPTIST. FROM A PHOTOGRAPH BY ALINARI AFTER THE FRESCO IN FLORENCE
IN THE CHIESA DI SANTA MARIA NOVELLA

Domenico Ghirlandaio
1449-1494

THE GOSPELS IN ART

THE BIRTH OF JOHN THE BAPTIST.   FROM A PHOTOGRAPH BY ALINARI AFTER
THE FRESCO IN THE CATHEDRAL AT SIENA

Bernardino Betto (il Pinturicchio)
1454-1513

THE VISIT OF MARY TO ELISABETH.   FROM A PHOTOGRAPH BY ALINARI AFTER THE FRESCO AT SIENA

Giovanni Antonio Bazzi (Sodoma)
1477-1549

The Childhood of Jesus Christ

THE BIRTH OF JESUS CHRIST. FROM A PHOTOGRAPH BY ANDERSON AFTER THE
PAINTING IN FLORENCE

Lorenzo di Credi
1459-1537

THE HOLY FAMILY. FROM A PHOTOGRAPH BY MESSRS. MANSELL AND CO. AFTER THE PICTURE IN
THE GLASGOW GALLERY

Tiziano Vecellio (Titian)
1477-1576

THE ADORATION OF THE SHEPHERDS. FROM A PHOTOGRAPH BY FRANZ HANFSTAENGL AFTER
THE PAINTING IN THE MUNICH GALLERY

Rembrandt van Rÿn

1606-1669

THE ANGEL OF THE LORD ANNOUNCING TO THE SHEPHERDS THE BIRTH OF JESUS CHRIST. FROM A CARBON PRINT BY
BRAUN, CLÉMENT & CO. AFTER THE PAINTING IN ROME

Jacopo da Ponte (Jacopo Bassano)

1510-1592

The Childhood of Jesus Christ

THE ADORATION OF THE SHEPHERDS. FROM A PHOTOGRAPH BY ANDERSON AFTER THE PICTURE IN THE
GALLERY OF ANCIENT AND MODERN ART, FLORENCE

Lorenzo di Credi

1459-1537

THE GOSPELS IN ART

THE ADORATION OF THE SHEPHERDS.   FROM A PHOTOGRAPH BY MESSRS. MANSELL AND CO.
AFTER THE PICTURE IN THE LOUVRE, PARIS

Josef de Ribera (Spagnoletto)
1588-1656

The Childhood of Jesus Christ

THE HOLY NIGHT. FROM A PHOTOGRAPH BY MESSRS. MANSELL AND CO. AFTER THE PAINTING IN
THE DRESDEN GALLERY

Antonio Allegri (Correggio)
1494-1534

THE ADORATION OF THE SHEPHERDS. FROM A PHOTOGRAPH BY HANFSTAENGL AFTER THE PICTURE IN VIENNA
Gerard van Honthorst

THE ADORATION OF THE SHEPHERDS. AFTER THE PICTURE IN THE PRADO, MADRID, FROM A PHOTOGRAPH
BY BRAUN, CLÉMENT AND CO., PARIS
Bartolomé Estéban Murillo
1618-1682

THE ARRIVAL OF THE SHEPHERDS.

REPRODUCED FROM A CARBON PRINT BY PERMISSION OF MESSRS. BRAUN, CLÉMENT & CO., PARIS

H. Lerolle

The Childhood of Jesus Christ

THE ADORATION CF THE SHEPHERDS.   REPRODUCED FROM THE ENGRAVING BY GAUTIER,
BY PERMISSION OF MESSRS. GOUPIL AND CO.

William Adolphe Bouguereau

THE GOSPELS IN ART

DURING THE NIGHT OF THE FIRST CHRISTMAS.   REPRODUCED FROM A PHOTOGRAVURE.   BY PERMISSION OF MESSRS. GOUPIL AND CO.

Louis Maurice Pierrey

"THE CHILDHOOD OF JESUS CHRIST

THE WISE MEN FROM THE EAST ON THEIR WAY TO BETHLEHEM.   REPRODUCED FROM THE ENGRAVING BY DUBOIS TESSELIN, BY PERMISSION OF HENRY GRAVES AND CO.

The Late Jean Portaels

THE NATIVITY.   REPRODUCED FROM A PHOTOGRAPH BY PERMISSION
OF FRED. HOLLYER, LONDON

Dante Gabriel Rossetti

1828-1882

THE NATIVITY.   AFTER THE PICTURE IN THE NATIONAL GALLERY, LONDON, FROM A PHOTOGRAPH BY FRANZ
HANFSTAENGL

Francesco Zurbaran

1598-1662

The Childhood of Jesus Christ

HE PRESENTATION IN THE TEMPLE.   FROM A PHOTOGRAPH BY FRANZ HANFSTAENGL AFTER THE PAINTING
IN THE BELVEDERE
VIENNA

Fra Bartolommeo (Baccio della Porta)
1475-1517

SIMEON IN THE TEMPLE.   FROM A PHOTOGRAPH BY HANFSTAENGL AFTER THE PICTURE AT THE HAGU

Rembrandt van Rÿn
1606-1669

THE CHILDHOOD OF JESUS CHRIST

THE PRESENTATION OF MARY IN THE TEMPLE. FROM A PHOTOGRAPH BY ANDERSON, ROME, AFTER THE
PAINTING IN THE VENICE ACADEMY

Tiziano Vecellio (Titian)
1477-1576

THE PRESENTATION OF THE VIRGIN. FROM A PHOTOGRAPH BY ALINARI AFTER THE FRESCO
AT SIENA IN THE ORATORIO DI S. BERNARDINO

Giovanni Antonio Bazzi (il Sodoma)
1477-1549

THE PRESENTATION IN THE TEMPLE. FROM A PHOTOGRAPH BY FRANZ HANFSTAENGL AFTER THE
PICTURE IN THE BRUSSELS GALLERY

Philippe de Champaigne

1602-1674

E ADORATION OF THE WISE MEN.   REPRODUCED FROM A PRINT KINDLY LENT BY MESSRS. MAGGS BROTHERS

Albrecht Dürer

1471-1528

THE CHILDHOOD OF JESUS CHRIST

MARY AND THE CHILD JESUS SURROUNDED BY HOLY INNOCENTS.   FROM A PHOTOGRAPH BY PERRIER
AFTER THE PICTURE IN THE LOUVRE

Peter Paul Rubens

1577-1640

THE ADORATION OF THE MAGI.   FROM A PHOTOGRAPH BY ANDERSON, ROME, AFTER THE PAINTING
FLORENCE IN THE UFFIZI GALLERY

Filippino Lippi

d. 1504

THE CHILDHOOD OF JESUS CHRIST

SIMEON: "LORD, NOW LETTEST THOU THY SERVANT DEPART IN PEACE." REPRODUCED FROM THE ENGRAVING BY J. J. CHANT, BY PERMISSION OF MESSRS. HENRY GRAVES AND CO.

William C. T. Dobson, R.A.

1817-1898

THE GOSPELS IN ART

THE ADORATION OF THE WISE MEN. FROM A PHOTOGRAPH BY BRAUN, CLÉMENT AND CO., PARIS, AFTER TH
DRAWING IN THE LOUVRE

Peter Paul Rubens
1577-1640

THE CHILDHOOD OF JESUS CHRIST

THE ADORATION OF THE WISE MEN. AFTER THE PICTURE IN THE PRADO FROM A PHOTOGRAPH
BY BRAUN, CLÉMENT AND CO., PARIS

Don Diego de Silva y Velazquez
1599-1660

THE HOLY FAMILY.   FROM A PHOTOGRAPH BY BRAUN, CLÉMENT AND CO., PARIS, AFTER THE PICTURE
IN THE PRADO, MADRID

Raffaello Sanzio (Raphael of Urbino)
1483-1520

The Childhood of Jesus Christ

ADORATION OF THE WISE MEN. REPRODUCED FROM THE ENGRAVING BY GAUTIER, BY PERMISSION OF MESSRS. GOUPIL AND CO.

William Adolphe Bouguereau

THE MADONNA OF THE MAGNIFICAT.   FROM A PHOTOGRAPH BY MESSRS. MANSELL AND CO., AFTER T
PICTURE AT PARIS IN THE LOUVRE

Sandro Botticelli

1447-1510

The Childhood of Jesus Christ

HE HOLY FAMILY. REPRODUCED FROM A PHOTOGRAPH BY FRANZ HANFSTAENGL AFTER THE PAINTING
AT FLORENCE IN THE UFFIZI GALLERY

Michelangelo Buonarroti

1475-1564

THE VIRGIN WITH THE HOLY CHILDREN ATTENDED BY AN ANGEL. FROM A PHOTOGRAPH BY
HANFSTAENGL AFTER THE PICTURE IN THE NATIONAL GALLERY, LONDON

Leonardo da Vinci

1452-1519

THE HOLY FAMILY.   FROM A PHOTOGRAPH BY PERRIER AFTER THE PICTURE IN THE MUSÉE DU LOUVRE

Simone Cantarini (il Pesarese)
1612-1648

HE HOLY FAMILY.   FROM A PHOTOGRAPH BY HANFSTAENGL AFTER THE PICTURE IN THE LIECHTENSTEIN
GALLERY, VIENNA

Nicolas Poussin
1594-1665

THE VIRGIN WITH THE CHILD JESUS AND JOHN THE BAPTIST. AFTER THE PICTURE IN THE ROYAL
GALLERY AT DRESDEN FROM A CARBON PRINT BY BRAUN, CLÉMENT AND CO., PARIS

Sandro Botticelli

1447-1510

THE MADONNA WITH THE INFANT JESUS. COPYRIGHT 1902 BY MESSRS. BRAUN, CLÉMENT & CO., PARIS

P. A. J. Dagnan-Bouveret

THE HOLY FAMILY OF FRANCIS I. OF FRANCE. AFTER THE PICTURE
IN THE LOUVRE FROM A PHOTOGRAPH BY THE AUTOTYPE CO.

Raphael
1483-1520

MARY AND THE CHILD JESUS. AFTER A MEZZOTINT BY C. TURNER
KINDLY LENT BY MR. F. B. DANIELL

Parmigia'no
1503-1540

The Gospels in Art.

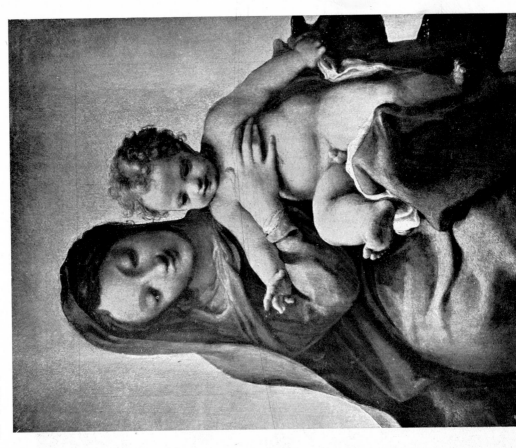

THE MADONNA OF ST. SEBASTIAN. AFTER THE PICTURE IN THE DRESDEN
GALLERY FROM A CARBON PRINT BY BRAUN, CLÉMENT AND CO., PARIS

Antonio Allegri da Correggio

THE HOLY FAMILY AND JOHN THE BAPTIST. AFTER A CARBON PRINT BY BRAUN,
CLÉMENT AND CO., PARIS, FROM THE PICTURE IN THE PRADO AT MADRID

Bernardino Luini

THE CHILDHOOD OF JESUS CHRIST

THE HOLY FAMILY RESTING ON THE WAY TO EGYPT. REPRODUCED AFTER A PHOTOGRAPH BY HANFSTAENGL

Anthony van Dyck

1599-1641

THE MASSACRE OF THE INNOCENTS. FROM A PHOTOGRAPH BY C. NAYA AFTER THE
PAINTING IN THE ACADEMY AT VENICE

Bonifacio Veronese (il Vecchio)
Died 1540

THE FLIGHT INTO EGYPT.   COPYRIGHT 1901 BY BRAUN, CLÉMENT & CO.

Jean Charles Cazin

THE FLIGHT INTO EGYPT.   COPYRIGHT 1901 BY BRAUN, CLÉMENT & CO.

Eugène Girardet

THE CHILDHOOD OF JESUS CHRIST

THE FLIGHT INTO EGYPT.   FROM A PHOTOGRAPH BY W. E. GRAY AFTER THE ORIGINAL DRAWING IN THE
POSSESSION OF THE CARFAX GALLERY, LONDON

William Blake
1757-1828

THE MASSACRE OF THE INNOCENTS. FROM A PHOTOGRAPH BY ANDERSON AFTER A TAPESTRY
IN THE VATICAN

Raffaello Sanzio (Raphael of Urbino)

1483-1520

THE CHILDHOOD OF JESUS CHRIST

THE FLIGHT INTO EGYPT. REPRODUCED FROM A PHOTOGRAPH BY BRAUN, CLÉMENT AND CO.

Alexandre Gabriel Decamps
1803-1860

E FLIGHT INTO EGYPT. AFTER A CARBON PRINT BY BRAUN, CLÉMENT AND CO. FROM THE ORIGINAL SKETCH

Jean François Millet
1814-1875

THE GOSPELS IN ART

THE FLIGHT INTO EGYPT

AFTER THE ORIGINAL ETCHING

THE TRIUMPH OF THE INNOCENTS.   REPRODUCED BY KIND PERMISSION FROM THE ORIGINAL PAINTING IN THE POSSESSION OF THE LIVERPOOL CORPORATION

William Holman Hunt

THE RETURN OF THE HOLY FAMILY TO NAZARETH.   REPRODUCED FROM THE ENGRAVING BY W. J. EDWARDS BY PERMISSION OF HENRY GRAVES AND CO.

THE CHILDHOOD OF JESUS CHRIST

THE CHILD JESUS QUESTIONING WITH THE DOCTORS.   AFTER
THE PICTURE AT NAPLES.   FROM A PHOTOGRAPH BY ALINARI

Salvatore Rosa
1615-1673

THE CHILD JESUS IN THE TEMPLE.   REPRODUCED FROM THE ENGRAVING BY J. J. CHANT BY PERMISSION
OF MESSRS. HENRY GRAVES AND CO.

William C. T. Dobson, R.A.
1817-1898

JOHN THE BAPTIST AS A CHILD. FROM A CARBON PRINT BY BRAUN, CLÉMENT AND CO., PARIS, FROM
THE PICTURE IN THE COLLECTION OF SIR FREDERICK COOK

Sir Joshua Reynolds, P.R.A.

1723-1792

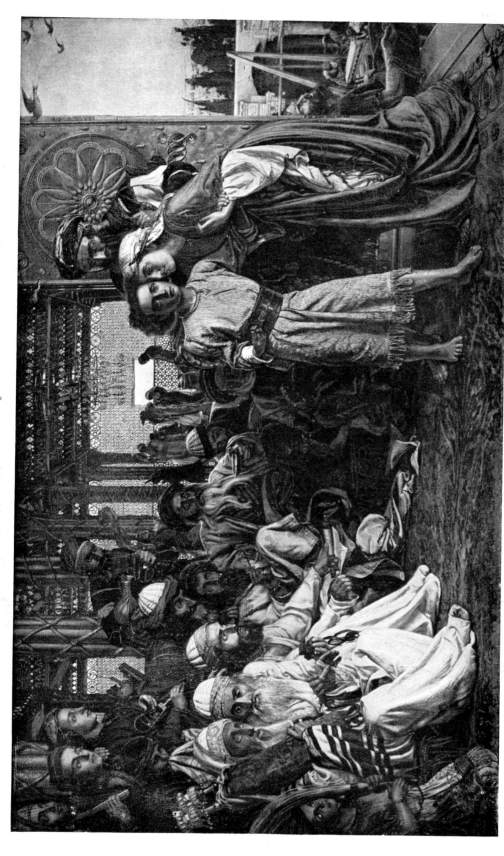

THE FINDING OF THE SAVIOUR IN THE TEMPLE.   REPRODUCED FROM THE PICTURE IN THE BIRMINGHAM GALLERY BY PERMISSION OF THE FINE ARTS COMMITTEE

William Holman Hunt

THE CHILDHOOD OF JESUS CHRIST

E CHILD JESUS IN THE TEMPLE QUESTIONING WITH THE DOCTORS.   FROM A PHOTOGRAPH BY ALINARI
AFTER THE FRESCO AT CREMONA IN THE CHIESA DI S. MARGHERITA

Giulio Campi
1500-1572

JESUS CHRIST MEETS JOHN THE BAPTIST.   AFTER A PHOTOGRAPH BY ALINARI FROM THE
ORIGINAL FRESCO IN THE CHIOSTRO DETTO DELLO SCALZO, FLORENCE

Franciabigio
1482-1525

THE CHILD JESUS AND THE DOCTORS.   AFTER A PHOTOGRAPH BY HANFSTAENGL FROM THE PICTUR
AT VIENNA

Josef de Ribera (Spagnoletto)
1588-1656

The Ministry of Jesus Christ

JERUSALEM AND THE VALLEY OF JEHOSHAPHAT. FROM THE PICTURE IN THE TATE GALLERY,
LONDON, AFTER A PHOTOGRAPH BY W. E. GRAY

Thomas Seddon
1821-1857

THE CHILD JESUS QUESTIONING WITH THE DOCTORS. REPRODUCED FROM THE TRANSLATOR'S-ETCHING
BY LÉON FLAMENG. BY PERMISSION OF MESSRS. SAMPSON LOW AND CO.

Alexandre Bida
1808-1895

THE GOSPELS IN ART

CHRIST IN THE HOUSE OF HIS PARENTS. EXHIBITED AT THE ROYAL ACADEMY IN 1850. REPRODUCED FROM AN ENGRAVING BY PERMISSION OF
MESSRS. HENRY GRAVES AND CO.

Sir J. E. Millais, Bart., P.R.A.

THE SHADOW OF DEATH.

The Ministry of Jesus Christ

By the Right Reverend G. A. Chadwick, D.D., Bishop of Derry and Raphoe

WHEN a thoughtful man examines a collection such as this, of the pictures in which great masters have striven to embody incidents of the earthly life of Jesus, he may be occupied in any of several ways. He may be only an artist studying art. Or again he may ask each picture for its message. What is here for me of thought or of emotion, concerning the Marriage of Cana, or the Transfiguration? So he may question one after another until he has exhausted the collection.

But there is more to be learned than one can see by treating them as independent units. Strange as the assertion may appear, and little as any of the workmen can have dreamed of this, their work has something in it of an organic unity, and the whole is greater than the sum of the parts.

Every worthy contributor to such a Gallery was a Student of the Sacred Life, as truly as any theologian of his day. He brought to his work the culture and thought of his time, and added whatever his own genius and piety could supply. The result sometimes, as we shall see, differed widely from the pronouncement of the theologians, and the difference is instructive; but even when it did not differ, it was the outcome of a totally different intellectual process.

The theologians were concerned with dogma: they searched for proof-texts: their supreme anxiety was to be orthodox. What we have in this volume is the result of many honest endeavours to "know Christ," to create for one's self and to show to others a real and worthy conception of Him, and of His acts when among us in the flesh.

The Gospels in Art

Did they succeed? Did they find heroism and majesty and tenderness, which it taxed and overtaxed all the resources of their art even to express? Was their noblest expression of these qualities attained by fidelity to the narrative or by self-willed endeavours to improve upon it? Did the greatest of them find here a theme for his greatest powers, or was his work upon this subject exceeded by what he did elsewhere? Did the characteristic knowledge and power of each race and age find here an adequate theme for its exertions? And is the result of this work, elaborated through many ages, coherent and progressive?

When we think of the matter thus, we perceive that the world's sacred pictures have many lessons beside the suggestions upon the surface of each canvas, being really a disclosure of the painter himself, and of his period, and of some at least of the message of the gospel not only to him but also to his age.

I

It was predicted of Jesus, as one aim and intention of His ministry, that "thoughts out of many hearts 'should' be revealed."

It was a great prediction. It is a gift of the highest natures only that they evoke what is essential in other men, and only the radically commonplace are commonplace when they are by.

Such this child should be. Where He should come deep would answer to deep. If there were any sort of nobility in a character, however overlaid and hidden, it would appear in his attitude toward Jesus, whom he would revere, even if he failed to worship Him.

Now this prediction has proved true. Saint or heretic, whatever anyone tells me about Christ, he tells me as much about himself; and there are passing phrases of Voltaire, Rousseau, and Strauss, which resemble finger-prints in a detective story, so inevitably do they betray the man. Every commentary upon His life has been an act of self-disclosure, a commentary also upon the commentator. So much and no more this man has prevailed to see and to tell us of the ideal greatness; and where his sympathy responded or his insight failed, we know, by this evidence, what manner of man he was. However flawed and blemished the external life, there was a heroic strain in everyone who could truly conceive of the Lord with His face steadfastly set to go up to Jerusalem, and purity and tenderness were in the thoughts of the hearts of everyone who understood His duplex utterance to the doomed woman whom He rescued,

"Go"—but go not back—"Go, and sin no more."

It is not to be denied that the four narratives—including St. John, and the miraculous quite as much as the didactic part of them—have this remarkable power upon the heart. They speak to it and it responds. Nay, they call to what is buried there, and it comes forth, perhaps like Lazarus, bound but living.

All this is true, in an emphatic sense, of those great commentators, the painters who have undertaken to embody for us in line and colour the dignity, the patience, the insight, the condescension, and the love of the Divine Man.

Let there be granted for the brush (as for the pen with which other commentators express themselves) grammar and vocabulary, that is to say, technical competence and power of utterance, and thereupon we find that all a man has within him is here evoked. Doré or Michael Angelo or Leonardo, French Sentimentalist or Pilgrim of Eternity, it is through the story of Jesus that they have striven, one and all, to utter what is deepest in them.

And this is vitally important. We are and ought to be impressed, when we find the same narratives which attract our foremost minds potent also with the Hottentot and the Eskimo. It is a noble evidence, which has never yet perhaps been elaborated as it deserves. But this is much more impressive, that the great artists of many centuries should have found in these same narratives the opportunity and suggestion of their finest work. It is a response to the gospel, and a confession of its power, from a direction utterly unthought of by the writers.

II

There is something more to say, for see what is implied in this incessant activity of art upon the gospel story. It brings each incident to the very severest test, the test of concrete embodiment. It proposes to give them, one after another, solidity, colour and form, flesh and blood. It sets the Master and the fallen woman, or leprous man, or anxious parent, and the disciples and the hostile critics, actually before our eyes. If the ideal in the Gospels were false or flawed, if any taint of insincere melodrama or undue self-assertion, anything too weak or too austere were in the story, here is the surest way possible to expose it. Nay, if the stories were only vague and nebulous, tendency legends, myths generated by impulses of which some are quite inconsistent with the mind of Christ in His teaching, the haze and the inconsistency could not be exposed more surely than by the attempt to give them form and body. From picture after picture the Master seems to say, "A spirit hath not flesh and bones, as ye see Me have."

Each great painting means that a highly trained student has been able to gaze with his mind's eye upon one incident in the sacred story, and has found it a coherent thing, and not only coherent but admirable. He has been able to place in the centre of each the Claimant to our Adoration; and to set Him there has not shaken the faith either of the painter or of us who gaze upon his work.

Even when such a picture fails in dignity or holiness, we are never conscious that the narrative is compromised, but that the work is inadequate : in our own minds we have another conception which is to this both the repudiation and the antidote.

Nor is it any reply to this argument that the same

THE PRODIGAL SON.

FROM THE ORIGINAL ETCHING

Alphonse Legros

men painted also Perseus and Andromeda. For they did not. They painted an ideal of beautiful and helpless womanhood and strong victorious manhood. You bring no such picture to the test of an authentic narrative; you quote no authority to justify or condemn it. The artist is also the inventor; and I have no quarrel with him if his Perseus is not mine. There is exactly the same difference as between history and a fairy tale. Moreover, the history is loftier than the tale, more inspiring, more pathetic. It is here only that the actual joins hands with the ideal. And as in life, so in art; the experiments of centuries, and of profound dissimilarities in temperament, education, and environment, are the witnesses that it does so.

III

The records of art are the picture galleries of the world. To pass from one master to another, from gallery to gallery, is to open the volumes of a great library, some written by contemporaries, others of widely different dates. And every age has its characteristics there disclosed, the thoughts of its heart are revealed. Not more clearly do we recognize mediæ-valism in the portrayal of St. John with a bishop's mitre, or St. Anna in the dress of a nun, than in its prevalent moods and aspirations. Even behind the galleries are the catacombs. And what contrast can be greater than between the simple and artless dignity of the Shepherd, bearing home the lost sheep, and the Light of the World, with nineteen centuries of baffled expecta-tion in His eyes, standing at midnight by a barred door? No one, looking at them for the first time, could possibly place them out of their true order. As we turn from one picture of Christ to another, and allow the meaning of each to sink down into our minds, it is as if the spirit of the period had come back to speak with us and to say how it conceived of Him. They are different, and they see Him differently, but they do not contradict each other; rather, there is nothing discerned by any which is not required for the completeness of the Perfect One, and much still remains for the future to teach our sons.

IV

All this is not enough to say. The Christ of art is not only the Revealer of the Secrets of each student and each period, He is their Instructor and Saviour also. Surprising indeed is the equipoise between these two characteristics of the story, that it is always near enough to every age to be comprehended ; and art shows each period busy in its own characteristic way upon this theme ; yet is it always far enough in advance to be a revelation and a guide ; and therefore we see also thoughts, hints, conjectures of the future. The story is sufficiently close to every age to be assimilated, but so potent that the assimilation is a chemical change. In many countries, throughout the dark ages, the best and most effectual teachers of the people were not the clergy, but, all unconsciously, the great masters who went straight to the Gospels for their inspiration and showed all men what they found there. Everywhere else was an asceticism which threatened to drain human nature of its heart's blood. Religion was not the purifying of our instincts, but their repression ; and to enter religion was to go into a monastery. The painters were themselves of the general opinion, as far as this was possible for men of genius who looked with sympathetic eyes upon nature and their fellow-men. We know how they conceived of saintship, for we can still see their Jeromes and Anthonies and Magdalenes. But what we have just seen, namely, that the man and the period are visible in their work, is not more certain than this, that the divine Subject overmastered both. It was possible to think of the saints as ascetics and even hermits ; possible, too, for art to find a very true nobility in that life which is consecrated for ever in the sublime and austere figure of the Baptist ; but the Perfect Man could not be thought of except mingling freely with

The Ministry of Jesus Christ

his fellows, eating and drinking with publicans and sinners.

The pictures of the Infancy proclaimed what the artists would hardly have been allowed to declare in words— the religious beauty of domestic life, the sacredness of those common ties which were blasphemed by current theories, the divinity of a baby's hand pressed to a mother's bosom. To paint the Holy Family was to declare that a family can be holy. Every such picture hung up in Church, and mingling its suggestions with the worship of the people, sank like rain into the ground in which lay hidden the germs of the Renaissance.

But it was not only the Infancy which taught such lessons. The whole life of Jesus was indeed obedient to legitimate authority, but it was independent of it and above it. It was a life, spiritually as well as physically, in the open air. It concerned itself with the whole range of human energy and feeling. Marriage and the shortcomings of a lowly menage, sickness, bereavement, frenzy, recovery of the incurable and even of the dead, controversy, popularity, desertion, friendship, and treason, the ideal life concerned itself with all of these, and even when the authorized teachers forgot this, the great artists did not fail to remember, and their works reminded the world that it was so.

A striking example is that celebrated Transfiguration by Raphael, to be found among the illustrations that follow this brief chapter.

It has always been observed that the "mountain" is represented as a mere hillock, in order to bring two groups into view together; above, the spectators of the "excellent glory," and below, the baffled disciples and the devil-tormented child. The contrast is indeed impressive. But it is even more suggestive. To the age of monasticism it said, What if the Master had consented to remain in rapt seclusion? What if Peter had been left where it was so "Good for 'him' to be," and allowed to build tabernacles there? Below, Satan would have vanquished the Church: the demon would never have been driven out.

It is so with the whole range of sacred Art. The great painter has looked for himself upon the world and upon the divine life ; and his picture tells us what he saw in both, and in their relations to each other. It is a self-revelation, and a revelation of his time, and a revelation of the mind of Him who governs the evolution of the ages.

George Derry & Raphoe .

FROM A COPYRIGHT PHOTOGRAPH BY BRAUN, CLÉMENT & Cº. PARIS.

SUFFER THE LITTLE CHILDREN TO COME UNTO ME.

The Ministry of Jesus Christ

JOHN THE BAPTIST PREACHING TO THE MULTITUDE. FROM A PHOTOGRAPH BY ALINARI
AFTER THE FRESCO AT FLORENCE IN THE CHIOSTRO DETTO DELLO SCALZO
Andrea del Sarto
1486-1531

BAPTISES THE MULTITUDE. FROM A PHOTOGRAPH BY ALINARI AFTER THE FRESCO IN THE SCALZO,
FLORENCE
Andrea del Sarto
1486-1531

The Gospels in Art

THE BAPTISM OF JESUS CHRIST. FROM A CARBON PRINT BY BRAUN, CLÉMENT AND CO., PARIS, AFT
THE PAINTING IN THE PRADO, MADRID

Jacopo Robusti (il Tintoretto)

1518-1594

THE MINISTRY OF JESUS CHRIST

HE BAPTISM OF JESUS CHRIST. AFTER A CARBON PRINT BY BRAUN, CLÉMENT AND CO., PARIS,
FROM THE PAINTING IN THE PITTI PALACE, FLORENCE

Paolo Caliari (Paolo Veronese)
1528-1588

THE GOSPELS IN ART

JOHN THE BAPTIST IN THE COUNTRY ABOUT JORDAN.
AFTER THE TRANSLATOR'S-ETCHING BY BRACQUEMOND,
BY PERMISSION OF MESSRS. SAMPSON LOW AND CO.

Alexandre Bida
1808-1895

THE BAPTISM OF JESUS CHRIST.   AFTER A PHOTOGRAPH BY ALINARI FROM THE FRESCO AT
FLORENCE IN THE CHIOSTRO DETTO DELLO SCALZO

Andrea del Sarto
1486-1531

JOHN THE BAPTIST. REPRODUCED FROM A PHOTOGRAPH OF THE ORIGINAL PAINTING BY PERMISSION
OF C. NAYA, VENICE

Tiziano Vecellio (Titian)

1477-1576

THE GOSPELS IN ART

THE SAVIOUR : FROM THE PAINTING OF THE TRIBUTE MONEY IN THE
PALAZZO BIANCO AT GENOA. REPRODUCED FROM A PHOTOGRAPH BY
ALINARI

Anthony van Dyck

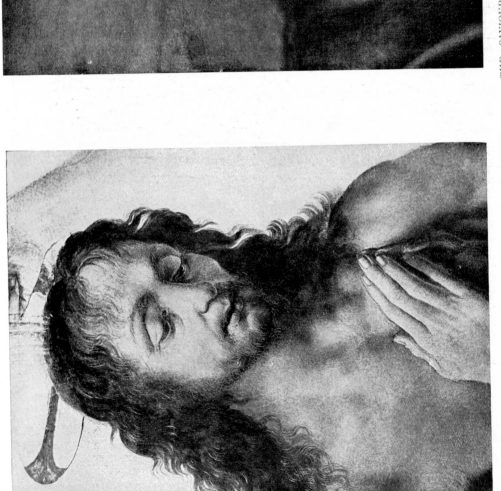

THE SAVIOUR : FROM THE PAINTING OF THE BAPTISM OF JESUS IN THE
GALLERY OF ANCIENT AND MODERN ART AT FLORENCE. AFTER A PHOTO-
GRAPH BY ALINARI

Andrea Verrocchio

THE MINISTRY OF JESUS CHRIST

THE TEMPTATION OF JESUS CHRIST. FROM A PHOTOGRAPH BY ANDERSON AFTER THE
PAINTING AT VENICE IN THE SCUOLA DI S. ROCCO

Jacopo Robusti (il Tintoretto)

1518-1594

JESUS CHRIST TEMPTED IN THE WILDERNESS. FROM A PHOTOGRAPH BY ALINARI AFTER THE
PICTURE AT NAPLES IN THE CASA MAGLIONE
Domenico Morelli

THE CALLING OF MATTHEW FROM THE RECEIPT OF CUSTOM. AFTER A CARBON PRINT BY FRANZ
HANFSTAENGL
Jan van Hemessen
Died between 1555-1566

THE MARRIAGE FEAST IN CANA OF GALILEE.

FROM A PHOTOGRAPH BY ALINARI AFTER THE PAINTING IN THE UFFIZI GALLERY, FLORENCE.

Jacopo Robusti (il Tintoretto)
1518-1594

THE MINISTRY OF JESUS CHRIST

THE CALLING OF ANDREW AND SIMON PETER. FROM A PHOTOGRAPH BY
FRANZ HANFSTAENGL AFTER THE PICTURE
IN THE BRUSSELS GALLERY

Federigo Barocci

1528-1612

The Gospels in Art

THE MARRIAGE FEAST IN CANA OF GALILEE. REPRODUCED FROM A PHOTOGRAPH BY PERMISSION OF W. A. MANSELL AND CO. AFTER THE
PAINTING AT PARIS IN THE MUSÉE DU LOUVRE

Paolo Caliari (Paolo Veronese)

THE MINISTRY OF JESUS CHRIST

JESUS CHRIST PURGING THE TEMPLE FOR THE FIRST TIME (ST. JOHN ii. 13-25).
FROM A PRINT LENT BY MESSRS. MAGGS BROTHERS

Rembrandt van Rÿn
1606-1669

ESUS CHRIST PURGING THE TEMPLE FOR THE FIRST TIME (ST. JOHN ii. 13-25). FROM A PHOTOGRAPH
BY ANDERSON AFTER THE PAINTING IN THE DORIA GALLERY, ROME

Jacopo Bassano
1510-1592

The Gospels in Art

JESUS CHRIST TALKING WITH THE WOMAN OF SAMARIA. FROM A PHOTOGRAPH
BY THE AUTOTYPE CO., NEW OXFORD STREET, AFTER THE PICTURE IN THE
TATE GALLERY

G. Richmond, R.A.
1809-1896

JESUS CHRIST AND THE WOMAN OF SAMARIA. REPRODUCED FROM A
PRINT KINDLY LENT BY MESSRS. MAGGS BROTHERS

Rembrandt van Rÿn
1606-1669

THE WOMAN OF SAMARIA.

REPRODUCED FROM THE PICTURE IN THE BIRMINGHAM GALLERY BY PERMISSION OF THE FINE ARTS COMMITTEE

William Dyce, R.A.

1806-1864

THE MINISTRY OF JESUS CHRIST

JOHN THE BAPTIST IN THE PRESENCE OF HEROD THE TETRARCH. FROM A PHOTOGRAPH BY ALINARI
AFTER THE FRESCO IN THE SCALZO, FLORENCE

Andrea del Sarto
1486-1531

" THE DAUGHTER OF HERODIAS DANCED BEFORE THEM AND PLEASED HEROD." AFTER A PHOTOGRAPH
BY ALINARI FROM THE FRESCO IN THE SCALZO, FLORENCE

Andrea del Sarto
1486-1531

THE GOSPELS IN ART

THE BEHEADING OF JOHN THE BAPTIST. FROM A PHOTOGRAPH BY BRAUN, CLÉMENT AND CO., PARIS, AFTER
THE PAINTING IN FLORENCE

Bernardino Luini

THE BEHEADING OF JOHN THE BAPTIST

The late Puvis de Chavannes

THE FIRST MIRACULOUS DRAUGHT OF FISHES. FROM A PHOTOGRAPH BY FRANZ HANFSTAENGL AFTER
THE PAINTING IN THE NATIONAL GALLERY, LONDON

Anthony van Dyck
1599-1641

THE SECOND MIRACULOUS DRAUGHT OF FISHES. FROM A PHOTOGRAPH BY FRANZ HANFSTAENGL AFT
THE PICTURE IN THE BRUSSELS GALLERY

Gaspard de Crayer
About 1582-1669

THE FIRST MIRACULOUS DRAUGHT OF FISHES. FROM A CARBON PRINT BY BRAUN, CLÉMENT AND CO. AFTER THE CARTOON IN THE
SOUTH KENSINGTON MUSEUM

Raffaello Sanzio (Raphael of Urbino)
1483-1520

THE GOSPELS IN ART

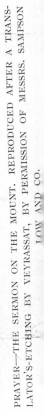

"ASK, AND IT SHALL BE GIVEN YOU." REPRODUCED FROM A TRANS-
LATOR'S-ETCHING BY FLAMENG, BY PERMISSION OF MESSRS. SAMPSON
LOW AND CO.

PRAYER.—THE SERMON ON THE MOUNT. REPRODUCED AFTER A TRANS-
LATOR'S-ETCHING BY VEYRASSAT, BY PERMISSION OF MESSRS. SAMPSON
LOW AND CO.

THE CENTURION OF CAPERNAUM BESEECHING CHRIST THAT HE WOULD COME AND HEAL HIS SERVANT. AFTER A CARBON PRINT BY BRAUN, CLÉMENT AND CO., FROM THE PAINTING IN THE ROYAL GALLERY, DRESDEN

Paolo Caliari (Paolo Veronese)
1528-1588

The Gospels in Art

THE SAVIOUR HEALING SIMON PETER'S WIFE'S MOTHER. FROM A PHOTOGRAPH
BY BRAUN, CLÉMENT AND CO. AFTER THE PICTURE IN THE LOUVRE

Paolo Caliari (Paolo Veronese)

THE SAVIOUR RAISING FROM THE DEAD THE WIDOW'S SON. FROM
AN ENGRAVING BY G. FOLO

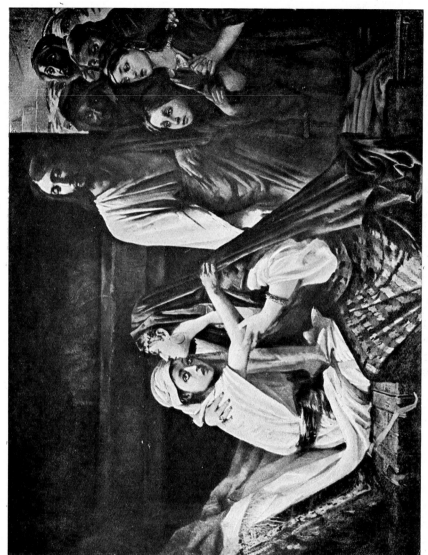

JESUS CHRIST RAISING FROM DEATH THE WIDOW'S SON. REPRODUCED FROM A PHOTOGRAPH BY
PERMISSION OF BRAUN, CLÉMENT AND CO., PARIS

Jean Jacques Scherrer

JESUS CHRIST HEALING THE SICK. REPRODUCED FROM A
PHOTOGRAPH BY BRAUN, CLÉMENT AND CO.

Joseph Aubert

JESUS CHRIST HEALING THE MAN AFFLICTED
WITH PALSY. AFTER A TRANSLATOR'S-ETCHING
BY HÉDOUIN. BY PERMISSION OF MESSRS.
SAMPSON LOW AND CO.

THE IMPOTENT MAN AT THE POOL OF B
ESDA. AFTER A TRANSLATOR'S-ETCHING E
NANTEUIL. BY PERMISSION OF MESSRS. SAM
LOW AND CO., LONDON

Alexandre Bida
1808-1895

JESUS CHRIST HEALING THE MAN WITH THE
WITHERED HAND. AFTER A TRANSLATOR'S-
ETCHING BY C. NANTEUIL. BY PERMISSION
OF MESSRS. SAMPSON LOW AND CO.

JESUS CHRIST HEALING TWO BLIND MEN. A
A TRANSLATOR'S-ETCHING BY L. FLAMENG.
PERMISSION OF MESSRS. SAMPSON LOW
CO., LONDON

Alexandre Bida
1808-1895

THE MINISTRY OF JESUS CHRIST

ARY MAGDALENE. FROM A PHOTOGRAPH BY ANDERSON, AFTER THE PAINTING AT NAPLES IN THE
NATIONAL MUSEUM

Tiziano Vecellio (Titian)

1477-1576

THE GOSPELS IN ART

MARY MAGDALENE IN THE HOUSE OF SIMON THE PHARISEE. FROM A PHOTOGRAPH BY BROGI AFTER THE PAINTING IN THE REALE
GALLERY, TURIN

THE MAGDALENE LAYING ASIDE HER JEWELS. AFTER A PHOTOGRAPH BY FRANZ HANFSTAENGL FROM THE PICTURE IN THE
NATIONAL GALLERY, LONDON

Paolo Caliari (Paolo Veronese)
1528-1588

THE GOSPELS IN ART

"BEHOLD, A SOWER WENT FORTH TO SOW; AND WHEN HE
SOWED, SOME SEEDS FELL BY THE WAY SIDE, AND THE FOWLS
CAME AND DEVOURED THEM UP." REPRODUCED
FROM AN OLD WOODCUT

"WHILE MEN SLEPT, HIS ENEMY CAME AND SOWED TARES AMONG THE WHEAT, AND WENT HIS
WAY." REPRODUCED FROM AN ENGRAVING BY FRANCISCUS KELLER, BY PERMISSION OF MESSRS
HENRY GRAVES AND CO.

Friedrich Overbeck

1789-1869

The Ministry of Jesus Christ

THE MERCHANTMAN AND THE PEARL OF GREAT PRICE. REPRODUCED FROM A PHOTOGRAPH
BY MESSRS. DIXON AND SON, LONDON

George W. Joy

THE GOSPELS IN ART

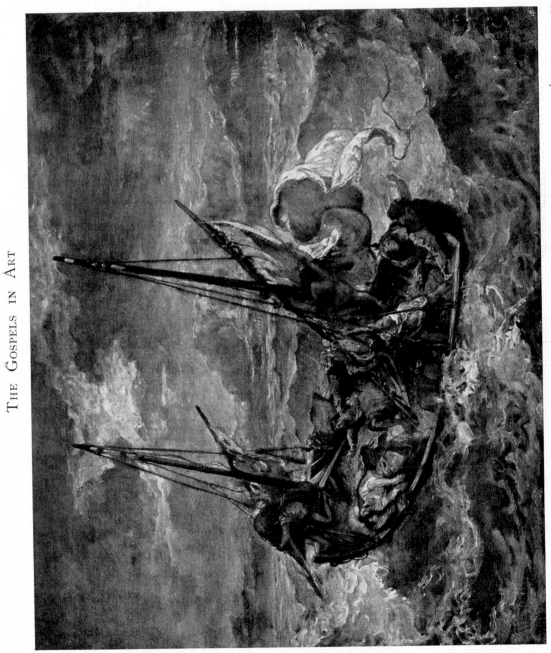

JESUS CHRIST SLEEPING IN THE TEMPEST ON THE SEA. AFTER A CARBON PRINT BY BRAUN, CLÉMENT AND CO.

Eugène Delacroix

THE MINISTRY OF JESUS CHRIST

THE MIRACLE OF THE GADARENE SWINE. REPRODUCED FROM A PHOTOGRAPH BY W. E. GRAY, LONDON, BY KIND PERMISSION OF
MESSRS. THOMAS AGNEW AND SONS, THE OWNERS OF THE COPYRIGHT

Briton Riviere, R.A.

The Gospels in Art

"AND HE SAID UNTO HER, DAUGHTER, THY FAITH HATH MADE THEE WHOLE; GO IN PEACE, AND
BE WHOLE OF THY PLAGUE," FROM A PHOTOGRAPH BY FRANZ HANFSTAENGL
AFTER THE PICTURE IN VIENNA

Paolo Caliari (Paolo Veronese)
1528-1588

THE MINISTRY OF JESUS CHRIST

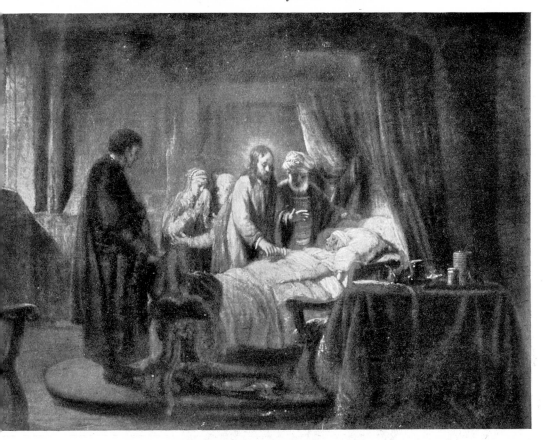

SUS CHRIST RAISING FROM DEATH JAIRUS' DAUGHTER. AFTER THE PICTURE IN BERLIN FROM A
PHOTOGRAPH BY HANFSTAENGL

G. van den Eeckhout
1621-1674

US CHRIST WALKING ON THE SEA. REPRODUCED FROM A PHOTOGRAVURE BY PERMISSION OF
MESSRS. GOUPIL AND COMPANY

Charles Jalabert
1819-1901

"AND IMMEDIATELY JESUS STRETCHED FORTH HIS
HAND AND CAUGHT HIM, AND SAID UNTO HIM, O
THOU OF LITTLE FAITH, WHEREFORE DIDST THOU
DOUBT?" FROM A PHOTOGRAPH BY BROGI AFTER
THE PICTURE IN THE NAPLES MUSEUM

Giovanni Lanfranco
1581-1647

JESUS CHRIST AND THE WOMAN OF CANAAN. FROM A PHOTOGRAPH BY ANDERSON AFTER THE
PAINTING IN THE ACADEMY AT VENICE

Jacopo Palma the Elder
1480-1528

REMBRANDT VAN RYN.

FROM A PHOTOGRAPH BY W. E. GRAY, AFTER A PROOF ETCHING IN THE BRITISH MUSEUM.

JESUS CHRIST PREACHING.

JESUS CHRIST PREACHING BY THE LAKE OF GENNESARETH. FROM A PHOTOGRAPH BY ALINARI
AFTER THE FRESCO AT CREMONA IN THE CHIESA DI S. MARGHERITA

Giulio Campi
1500-1572

THE GOSPELS IN ART

JESUS CHRIST HEALING THE SICK. FROM A PHOTOGRAPH BY BRAUN, CLÉMENT AND CO., PARIS, AFTER THE PICTURE IN BUCKINGHAM PALACE

JESUS CHRIST HEALING THE SICK. FROM A PHOTOGRAPH BY THE AUTOTYPE CO., NEW OXFORD STREET, LONDON, AFTER THE HUNDRED
GUILDER PRINT

Rembrandt van Rÿn
1606-1669

THE TRANSFIGURATION.   FROM A PHOTOGRAPH BY W. A. MANSELL AND CO. AFTER THE PAINTING AT RO
IN THE VATICAN

Raffaello Sanzio (Raphael of Urbino)
1483-1520

THE TRANSFIGURATION. AFTER THE PAINTING IN THE NATIONAL MUSEUM, NAPLES, FROM A PHOTOGRAPH BY FRANZ HANFSTAENGL, LONDON AND MUNICH

Giovanni Bellini

d. 1516

The Ministry of Jesus Christ

"AND WHOSO SHALL RECEIVE ONE SUCH LITTLE CHILD IN MY NAME RECEIVETH ME." AFTER A
CARBON PRINT BY BRAUN, CLÉMENT AND CO., FROM THE CARTOON IN THE MUSÉE DE LYON

Paul Chenavard
Died 1895

THE GOSPELS IN ART

JESUS CHRIST AND THE CONDEMNED, FALLEN WOMAN.   AFTER A CARBON PRINT BY BRAUN, CLÉMENT AND CO. FROM THE
PICTURE IN THE COLLECTION OF THE DUKE OF WESTMINSTER

"NEITHER DO I CONDEMN THEE : GO, AND SIN NO MORE."
FROM A PHOTOGRAPH BY BRAUN, CLÉMENT AND CO., PARIS

A. A. Anderson

MARY OF BETHANY. FROM A PHOTOGRAPH BY MESSRS. DIXON AND SON

G. W. Joy

"AND AGAIN HE STOOPED DOWN AND WROTE ON THE GROUND." REPRODUCED FROM AN ETCHIN
BY HÉDOUIN, BY PERMISSION OF MESSRS. SAMPSON LOW AND CO.

Alexandre Bida
1808-1895

JESUS CHRIST WITH MARTHA AND MARY. REPRODUCED AFTER THE PICTURE IN AMSTERDAM FROM
PHOTOGRAPH BY FRANZ HANFSTAENGL

Flemish School

THE MINISTRY OF JESUS CHRIST

JESUS CHRIST AND THE SISTERS OF BETHANY. REPRODUCED FROM AN
ENGRAVING BY M. I. DANFORTH

Charles Robert Leslie, R.A.
1794-1859

JESUS CHRIST IN THE HOUSE OF MARTHA AND MARY. AFTER THE PICTURE IN THE LOUVRE FROM
A CARBON PRINT BY BRAUN, CLÉMENT AND CO., PARIS

Hendrick van Steenwyck the Younger
About 1580-after 1649

THE LIGHT OF THE WORLD.   AFTER A PHOTOGRAPH BY THE AUTOTYPE CO
NEW OXFORD STREET, LONDON

W. Holman Hunt

THE MINISTRY OF JESUS CHRIST

HE SAVIOUR. FROM A PHOTOGRAPH BY BRAUN, CLÉMENT AND CO. AFTER THE PAINTING AT FLORENCE
IN THE PITTI PALACE

Tiziano Vecellio (Titian)
1477-1576

THE GOOD SAMARITAN. FROM A CARBON PRINT BY BRAUN, CLÉMENT AND CO., AFTER THE PICTUR
IN THE LOUVRE

Rembrandt van Rÿn
1606-1669

THE PARABLE OF THE GOOD SAMARITAN. AFTER THE DRAWING IN THE COLLECTION OF OTTO S. ANDREAE,

Abraham van Diepenbeeck
1596-1675

"If Thou Hadst Known"

William Hole, R.S.A.

REPRODUCED FROM THE ORIGINAL ETCHING

The Ministry of Jesus Christ

JESUS CHRIST LAMENTING OVER JERUSALEM. AFTER A PHOTOGRAPH BY THE AUTO-
TYPE CO. FROM THE PICTURE IN THE TATE GALLERY
Sir C. L. Eastlake, P.R.A.
1793-1866

JESUS CHRIST AND THE PHARISEES. FROM A PHOTOGRAPH BY THE AUTOTYPE CO., NEW OXFORD ST.,
LONDON, AFTER THE PAINTING IN THE NATIONAL GALLERY
Bernardino Luini
About 1475-after 1533

THE GOSPELS IN ART

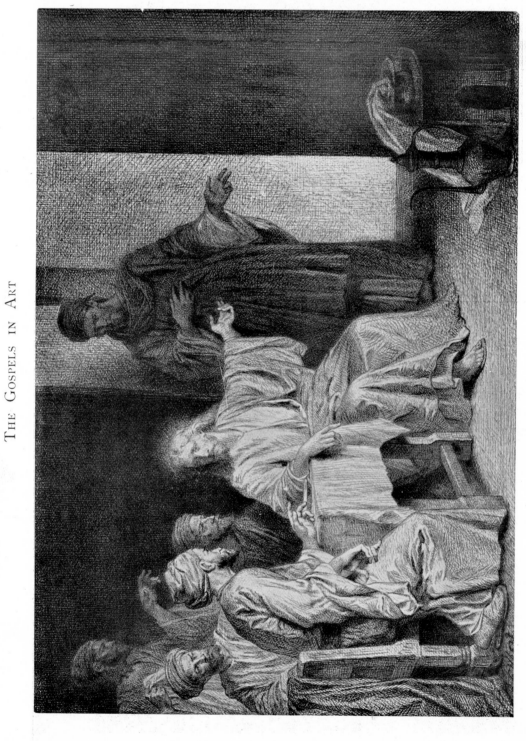

JESUS CHRIST HEALING THE MAN WITH DROPSY IN THE HOUSE OF ONE OF THE CHIEF PHARISEES. REPRODUCED FROM AN ETCHING
BY GILBERT BY PERMISSION OF MESSRS. SAMPSON LOW AND CO.

Alexandre Bida

THE MINISTRY OF JESUS CHRIST

The parable of the lost piece of money

REPRODUCED FROM A PROOF ENGRAVING BY W. H. SIMMONS BY PERMISSION OF
MESSRS. HENRY GRAVES AND CO.

Sir John Everett Millais, P.R.A.
1829-1896

THE GOSPELS IN ART

THE PRODIGAL SON: "AND WHEN HE HAD SPENT ALL." AFTER THE ORIGINAL ETCHING

Sir Charles Holroyd

THE PRODIGAL SON: "AND TOOK HIS JOURNEY INTO A FAR COUNTRY, AND THERE WASTED HI
SUBSTANCE WITH RIOTOUS LIVING." AFTER A CARBON PRINT BY BRAUN, CLÉMENT AND CO. AFTE
THE PICTURE IN PARIS IN THE LOUVRE

David Teniers the Younger

1610-1690

THE RETURN OF THE PRODIGAL SON.   FROM A PHOTOGRAPH BY FRANZ HANFSTAENGL AFTER THE PICTURE AT VIENNA
IN THE ROYAL GALLERY

Pompeo Girolamo Batoni

1708-1787

THE PRODIGAL SON.   REPRODUCED AFTER A PHOTOGRAPH BY FREDERICK HOLLYER,
LONDON

G. F. Watts, R.A.
1817-1904

THE PRODIGAL SON.   REPRODUCED AFTER A PHOTOGRAPH BY FRED.
HOLLYER

G. F. Watts, R.A.
1817-1904

186

THE GOSPELS IN ART

THE RETURN OF THE PRODIGAL SON. AFTER THE PICTURE IN ST. PETERSBURG
FROM A PHOTOGRAPH BY HANFSTAENGL

THE PRODIGAL SON. REPRODUCED FROM A PHOTOGRAPH BY PERMISSION
OF BRAUN, CLÉMENT AND CO., PARIS

187

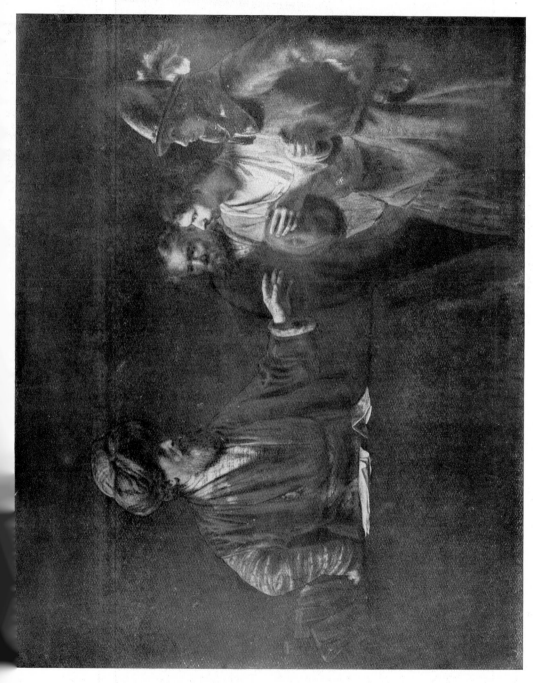

THE UNMERCIFUL SERVANT. REPRODUCED AFTER THE PAINTING IN THE WALLACE COLLECTION, LONDON, FROM A
PHOTOGRAPH BY W. A. MANSELL AND CO.

Rembrandt van Rÿn
1606-1669

188

THE GOSPELS IN ART

THE PARABLE OF THE RICH MAN AND THE BEGGAR NAMED LAZARUS. FROM A PHOTOGRAPH BY ANDERSON AFTER THE PAINTING IN THE VENICE ACADEMY

Bonifazio Veronese the Elder
16th Century

The Parable of the Great Supper: "Then the Master of the house being angry said to his servant, go out quickly into the streets and lanes of the city, and bring in hither the poor and the maimed, and the halt, and the blind." Reproduced from a carbon print by permission of Messrs. Braun, Clément & Co., Paris

Eugène Burnand

THE PARABLE OF THE BLIND LEADING THE BLIND. FROM A PHOTOGRAPH BY FRANZ HANFSTAENGL AFTER THE PICTURE IN THE NATIONAL MUSEUM IN NAPLES

Peter Breughel the Elder
about 1525-1569

DVCAM VOS DESEPVLCRIS POPVLVS MEVS. EÇECHIEL. XXXVII. C.

CIAMNIT YHS VOCE MAĜ IACERE VENI FORAS. 7 STATIM PRODIIT Q ERAT MORTVVS. IO. II. C.

L. AIAMINI MVNDI ESTOE AVFERE MALVM COGITATIONVM VESTRARVM. YSAIE. I. C.

THE RESURRECTION OF LAZARUS. FROM A PHOTOGRAPH BY ANDERSON AFTER THE TEMPERA
PAINTING AT FLORENCE IN THE GALLERY OF ANCIENT AND MODERN ART

Fra Giovanni Angelico da Fiesole

1387-1455

HE RAISING OF LAZARUS, THE BROTHER OF MARTHA AND MARY OF BETHANY. FROM A PHOTOGRAPH
BY FRANZ HANFSTAENGL AFTER THE PAINTING IN THE BERLIN GALLERY

Peter Paul Rubens
1577-1640

JESUS CHRIST RECEIVING LITTLE CHILDREN. FROM A PHOTOGRAPH BY BROGI AFTER THE PAINTING
AT FLORENCE IN THE ACADEMY OF FINE ARTS

Pietro Benvenuti

THE LORD OF THE VINEYARD PAYING HIS LABOURERS.   AFTER A MEZZOTINT BY WILLIAM PETHER KINDLY LENT BY
MR. F. B. DANIELL

Rembrandt van Ryn

1606-1669

"FOR OF SUCH IS THE KINGDOM OF HEAVEN." AFTER A PHOTOGRAPH BY W. A. MANSELL AND CO. FROM THE PICTURE IN THE MANCHESTER ART GALLERY

Sir C. L. Eastlake, P.R.A.
1793-1866

"HE WENT AWAY SORROWFUL FOR HE HAD GREAT POSSESSIONS." REPRODUCED FROM A PHOTOGRAPH BY PERMISSION OF FRED. HOLLYER, LONDON, AFTER THE PICTURE IN THE TATE GALLERY

George Frederick Watts, R.A.
1817-1904

The Ministry of Jesus Christ

"BLESSED ARE THE POOR." REPRODUCED FROM A PHOTOGRAVURE BY PERMISSION OF GOUPIL AND CO.

Léon Augustin Lhermitte

ЕSUS CHRIST INSTRUCTING THE YOUNG MAN HOW TO ATTAIN ETERNAL LIFE. REPRODUCED FROM AN
ENGRAVING BY PERMISSION OF HENRY GRAVES AND CO.

Henry Le Jeune, A.R.A.

THE GOSPELS IN ART

THE PARABLE OF THE LABOURERS IN THE VINEYARD. FROM A PHOTOGRAPH BY FRANZ HANFSTAENGL AFTER THE PAINTING AT
ST. PETERSBURG IN THE HERMITAGE GALLERY

Rembrandt van Rÿn

THE TRIBUTE MONEY: BUT HE PERCEIVED THEIR CRAFTINESS, AND SAID UNTO THEM, WHY TEMPT YE ME? SHEW ME
A PENNY. (ST. LUKE XX. 23-24). AFTER THE PICTURE IN THE DRESDEN GALLERY FROM A CARBON PRINT
BY BRAUN, CLÉMENT & CO.

Tiziano Vecellio (Titian)

1477-1576

THE MINISTRY OF JESUS CHRIST

E ENTRY OF JESUS CHRIST INTO JERUSALEM. REPRODUCED FROM A PHOTOGRAVURE BY PERMISSION
OF MESSRS. GOUPIL AND CO., PARIS

J. L. Gérôme
1824-1904

HE ENTRY OF JESUS CHRIST INTO JERUSALEM. REPRODUCED AFTER THE ENGRAVING BY GAUTIER
BY PERMISSION OF MESSRS. GOUPIL AND CO.

Edouard Dubufe
1820-1883

THE HEALING OF THE BLIND IN JERICHO. AFTER THE PICTURE IN ST. PETERSBURG, FROM A
PHOTOGRAPH BY HANFSTAENGL
Lucas van Leyden
1494-1533

JESUS CHRIST AND THE FRUITLESS LEAFY TREE. REPRODUCED AFTER AN ETCHING BY PERMISSION
OF MESSRS. SAMPSON LOW AND CO.
Alexandre Bida
1808-1895

The Ministry of Jesus Christ

SIMON PETER FINDS THE PIECE OF TRIBUTE MONEY IN THE
MOUTH OF THE FISH. AFTER THE PAINTING IN ANTWERP

Martin de Vos
1532-1603

THE GOSPELS IN ART

THE WIDOW'S MITE. FROM A CARBON PRINT BY BRAUN,
CLÉMENT AND CO. AFTER THE PAINTING IN THE ANTWERP
MUSEUM

Martin de Vos
1532-1603

Rembrandt van Rÿn

1606-1669

THE PARABLE OF THE FIVE WISE AND FIVE FOOLISH VIRGINS.   REPRODUCED FROM A PHOTOGRAPH BY PERMISSION OF
THE FINE ARTS COMMITTEE OF THE BIRMINGHAM ART GALLERY

W. J. Wainwright, A.R.W.S.

ONE OF THE FOOLISH VIRGINS. AFTER A PHOTOGRAPH BY W. A. MANSELL
AND CO. FROM THE PICTURE IN THE MANCHESTER ART GALLERY

Valentine Cameron Prinsep, R.A.

Born 1836—Elected R.A. 1894

THE FIVE FOOLISH VIRGINS. REPRODUCED FROM AN ETCHING BY
PERMISSION OF MESSRS. SAMPSON LOW AND CO.

Alexandre Bida

1808-1895

JESUS CHRIST. FROM A CARBON PRINT BY BRAUN, CLÉMENT AND CO., AFTER THE PAINTING IN THE COLLECTION OF M. CHARLES SEDELMEYER, PARIS

Rembrandt van Rÿn

1606-1669

The Ministry of Jesus Christ

JESUS CHRIST. REPRODUCED FROM A COPYRIGHT PHOTOGRAPH BY PERMISSION OF FRED. HOLLYER, LONDON

Dante Gabriel Rossetti

1828-1882

214

THE GOSPELS IN ART

THE LAST SUPPER OF JESUS CHRIST WITH THE TWELVE APOSTLES. FROM A PHOTOGRAPH BY THE AUTOTYPE CO., NEW OXFORD STREET, LONDON, AFTER THE ENGRAVING BY RAPHAEL MORGHEN

Leonardo da Vinci
1452-1519

THE LAST SUPPER OF JESUS CHRIST WITH THE TWELVE APOSTLES. AFTER A PHOTOGRAPH BY ANDERSON OF THE PAINTING AT VENICE IN
SAN GIORGIO MAGGIORE

Jacopo Robusti (il Tintoretto)
1518-1594

THE GOSPELS IN ART.

FROM THE PICTURE IN THE MUSÉE DU LOUVRE

Philippe de Champaigne

THE LAST SUPPER WITH THE TWELVE APOSTLES

CHRIST AND ST. JOHN. FROM THE FRESCO OF THE LAST SUPPER IN THE CENECOLO DI FOLIGNO, FLORENCE. REPRODUCED FROM A PHOTOGRAPH BY ANDERSON, ROME

Attributed to Raphael

THE GOSPELS IN ART

JESUS CHRIST WASHING ST. PETER'S FEET. FROM A PHOTOGRAPH BY FRANZ HANFSTAENGL AFTER
THE PICTURE IN THE TATE GALLERY

Ford Maddox Brown

FROM A PHOTOGRAPH BY BRAUN & CLÉMENT, PARIS. BY PERMISSION OF M. CHARLES SEDELMEYER.

JESUS CHRIST BEFORE PILATE.

From Gethsemane to Olivet

By Robert F. Horton, M.A., D.D.

T is evident that the trial, the torture, and the execution of a prisoner is not a fit subject for Art; and if the scene be placed among a people of fierce and ruthless fanaticism, controlled by a government that employs scourging and crucifixion as judicial penalties, it might be supposed that Art would instincitively shrink from the subject matter which is thus presented. It has been shown that the Laocoon violates the principles which should regulate the art of sculpture, because the permanence of marble is unsuitable for the expression of a writhing and distorted passion. But a similar principle would forbid to the sister art of painting the delineation of brutal and unnecessary torments.

It is therefore a surprising fact that some of the greatest masters of painting, in the greatest periods of their art, have occupied themselves with the subject of the punishment of Jesus.

Now, if such a subject is to be treated successfully, there must be in the painter's mind an intellectual purpose or a spiritual penetration, or a combination of the two, which can dominate its physical sufferings, and justify the choice of the subject. It is for example a mere *tour de force* when Rembrandt in his *Butcher's Shop* claims our attention for the opened and outstretched carcass of a sheep, which, if it were there in reality, would be only disgusting. The painter's triumph consists in such a handling of the light and shadow that the reds and yellows of the carcass present an agreeable scheme of colour. But when the same painter, in his *School of Medicine* at The Hague, lays before us a dead body under dissection, and lights up his picture with the livid white of the skin and the red patch of the opened arm, he counteracts the displeasing and even distressing impression of the corpse by the circle of interested and intellectual faces gathered around the dissecting table. The doctors in their sober dress, intensely absorbed in their subject of study, do not allow the observer for a moment to forget that the dead body is there only in the interest of science, and that science is pursued only in the cause of mercy. The intensity of the intellectual and spiritual interests subdues the physical fact of death to a subordinate and incidental position, allowing the painter to use the pallor of the limbs and the red of the blood as elements of beauty in the picture.

In dealing therefore with the passion of Christ, the artist must be judged by the way in which he is able to penetrate into the significance of the event, and make the spiritual reality, which underlies the sordid physical facts, manifest and impressive to the spectator.

For instance, if he is conscious of the pathos which lies in the punishment meted out to disturbing enthusiasms by the rigid order of the world, he can breathe into his treatment of the crucifixion that tender and piquant sorrow which is excited, let us say, by the story of Joan of Arc. But a painter would not carry us along with him if he represented the Maid of Domrémy subjected to the brutalities of a coarse soldiery, or if he in any way emphasised the tortures of the flames in the market-place of Rheims. That an innocent and beautiful enthusiast should die at the hands of the world, is a proper study for the artist, but it is no excuse for obtruding upon our notice the details of the suffering, which are in themselves merely repulsive. The justification for handling the death of Jesus, in the way Art has attempted to handle it, must be sought in some idea which goes much further than that of an innocent sufferer who is the victim of the world's prejudices or of governmental expediencies. This idea, which goes much further, and which alone justifies the artistic treatment of the Passion, is, it need hardly be said, the truth that Christ's sufferings were the means of the world's redemption. He was despised and rejected of men, a man of sorrows and acquainted with grief, because the chastisement of the world's peace was upon Him ; He was numbered with the transgressors, because He bore the sins of many. He suffered the brutalities of the soldiers and anguish of the Cross, because to pour out His soul unto death was the means of saving not only the world at large, but even those who scourged and slew Him ; the bitter cry, "My God! why hast Thou forsaken Me?" indicates the central fact of an atoning sacrifice ; and the triumphant issue from the tomb is the outward evidence that the sacrifice was complete and accepted, and that He had opened the Kingdom of Heaven to all believers. When the real nature of these transactions is understood, when the process is removed as it were from the petty court of a provincial government into the course and crisis of a world's salvation, every detail of that last scene, from the Supper with the disciples to the appearance three days later in the Upper Room, becomes of absorbing interest. With an instinctive perception of what the Passion meant, the Evangelists give one-fourth of their narratives to the subject, though they hardly venture to make any comment or to point the meaning of the events.

Now if Art is to deal successfully with this theme, the artists must be inspired by the true idea, and the success of each must be estimated by the degree in which he impresses the spectator with that idea. No one has any business to be painting any incident in the Passion of Christ who has not apprehended who it is that is suffering, and what He is suffering for. True, it is a man, Jesus of Nazareth, the rejected Prophet of Galilee, who is scourged in the Pretorium, and crucified at Calvary ; but the painter has no excuse for representing these events unless he sees God in the man. The sufferings, as the mere penalties of a broken human law, are commonplace and insignificant ; it is no business of the artist to rake among the sordid brutalities of the past and to show how the pitiless masters of the world nailed their fugitive slaves to crosses. The artist can only treat this subject if he has caught a glimpse of the truth that the Sufferer bore our sins in His own body on the tree, was crucified for our redemption, and raised again for our justification.

223

The Gospels in Art

There is a picture of the crucified One in the gallery at Dusseldorf which has a lasting interest for the world, because it arrested the young Count Zinzendorf, and with its inscription, " I did this for thee, what hast thou done for Me? " moved him to his life of singular and successful devotion. But the painter of that picture had reached his design only after repeated failures. When he had first painted the face of Christ he asked a little child what she thought of it; she said, " That is a good man," and the artist knew that he had failed. He tried again, and the child was moved with pity for the sufferer; again the painter knew that he had failed. Then he gave himself to prayer, that he might know what the Lord's face was like; and this time, when the child came into the studio, she fell upon her knees, and knew that she was in the presence of Christ.

The test then in the treatment of this subject cannot be merely artistic; or rather, to be artistic here the artist must be something more, he must have faith, he must have spiritual insight. It is impossible to deal artistically with the Passion of Christ unless he sees in it the offering of a sacrifice for the salvation of the world. Some years ago the Hungarian painter, Munkacsy, exhibited a picture of the Crucifixion, the avowed object of which was to show us the scene in all its sordid realism. There was the sufferer, indistinguishable from His fellow sufferers, and on a level with His executioners and tormentors. As a piece of realism it was admirable, and the technical handling was skilful enough, but the inevitable remark which sprang to the lips of the spectator was this: If the painter had seen or could see in the event nothing more, what right had he to inflict it upon us? We do not wish to study in the name of Art the human shambles of nineteen centuries ago. What concern have we to see these ragged and dirty Jewish felons writhing under the gaze of a few fanatical rulers and a band of callous soldiery? Either the painter should have seen more or he should have withheld his hand.

It does not always mean that the painter must be in spiritual harmony with his theme; all that is meant is that

ECCE HOMO: PILATE PRESENTING JESUS CHRIST TO THE PEOPLE.   AFTER A PHOTOGRAPH BY MESSRS. MANSELL
& COMPANY

Antonio Allegri da Correggio

1494-1534

he must be in imaginative or artistic sympathy with the spiritual significance of it, or he cannot artistically treat the Passion of Christ. Guido Réni was probably but little moved by the Christian verities, and he worked in that bad time when the Renaissance was crumbling into corruption and decay, but his painting of the Crucifixion in San Pietro in Carcere satisfies the demand we are now making; for that white form lifted high between the earth and the heavens, outlined against the stormy sky and against the background where the guilty city lay, is obviously the sacrifice of earth to heaven, the Lamb of God which taketh away the sins of the world; the intellectual and spiritual considerations entirely dominate the physical fact, and Art has found its function in interpreting the reality which might have escaped the commonplace observer of the scene.

Again Sodoma was, it is to be feared, no exemplary Christian, and his understanding of spiritual things cannot be derived from the living of a spiritual life; but his imaginative sympathy with the religious trouble of his time enabled him to paint his picture of Christ leaving the tomb in the Palazzo Publico, at Siena. The very spirit of the Resurrection has entered into the composition; the Lord issues from the grave above the sleeping guards in the clear cold light of the morning, with such a mien and port as indicate at once that it was impossible that death should have held Him. The difficulties of the situation, and of presenting a body which has been dead emerging from the sepulchre, are overcome by the master thought, realized at least artistically, that this event is the pledge and the potency of the resurrection of mankind. No eye beheld Him rising from the grave, and what the eye has not seen it may be presumptuous for a painter to depict. It was easy to make a fiasco, and on the principles of realism in Art a fiasco would have been certain; but the event was viewed in its spiritual aspect, and the spiritual impression is conveyed by the plastic forms and by the atmosphere of the painting.

But to deal quite worthily with the theme we must have painters who enter into the situation by a spiritual faith,

227

and not only by a sympathetic imagination. Such painters appeared in Italy at the point where the simple piety of mediævalism was blooming, and not yet blighted by the pagan influences of the Renaissance. Perugino in Umbria, Fra Angelico in Florence, and Giovanni Bellini in Venice, were able to present the Passion of our Lord with complete sincerity ; the spiritual truth mastered the physical details, and the Agony in the Garden, and the bloody anguish of the Cross presented themselves on those glowing canvases not as the hideous incidents of a brutal tragedy, but as what they really were, the outward and visible signs of that transaction in the spiritual world by which humanity is reconciled to God.

Among modern artists there are some who are able to approach the theme with the same sincerity and conviction. The Pre-Raphaelite Brotherhood, with all its self-consciousness and suggestion of affectation, at least produced Holman Hunt ; and no mediæval painter in the Agony of the Garden or the Crucifixion ever more faithfully represented the Passion of our Lord than Holman Hunt has done, symbolically, in his incomparable picture of the Scapegoat. He shrank, perhaps, from attempting a direct presentation of the Passion. Who might not, after the gross and carnal vulgarities which have been perpetrated by the materialistic religion, and the histrionic art of the modern world ? But the Scapegoat is Holman Hunt's surety that Art will yet attempt to represent worthily the greatest scene in the drama of humanity. What the four Evangelists accomplished in literature by their absolute sincerity, moved no doubt unconsciously by the breath of the Spirit, waits yet to be accomplished in Art. The mediæval method and spirit are no longer suitable to the human mind. The facts of nature and the facts of humanity war against them, and the modern artist who attempted to work in the manner of Bellini, Fra Angelico, or Perugino, would produce no conviction, because he could not himself be convinced. But the time will come when the facts of the Gospels will harmonize with all our knowledge, whether of the world or of man, and then the artist who has brain and heart enough will be able to throw himself into the task of delineating to the eye what the Evangelists delineated to the mind. He will be able to paint the Lord's Supper, the Agony in the Garden, the appearance before the High Priest or before Pilate, the Scourging, and the Ecce Homo, the Cross and all its incidents, the Resurrection and the several appearances of the risen Lord, in a way which will show their relation to all the life of the soul and to all the hopes of man. The great efforts of the past will not be discredited, but they will be transcended; and a later generation will wonder how we were ever content with the superficial and childish representations of the stupendous events which fixed the destiny and determined the developement of the race of men.

In the little church of a Norfolk village there is a baptismal font adorned with crude and primitive sculptures. Facing the altar, from which Sunday by Sunday the Commandments are read forbidding us to make images of the Divine, is a rude representation of the Holy Trinity; God the Father sits upon a throne, and holds between His knees Christ upon the Cross, while between His chin and the top of the Cross is the Holy Ghost in the image of a dove. The whole composition appears to the modern eye like a grotesque blasphemy; and one could hardly be surprised if the children baptized in that font, and brought up in sight of such an image of Him who fills Heaven and Earth, should grow into sceptics. The mode in which the supreme mystery of our Lord's Passion has been handled in Europe may be responsible for some of that surprising godlessness which is to be met with in the modern world. If Christ was in any sense God, if His sufferings implied that there was the Divine love bearing the sin of the world, to present that sublime transaction in a crude or unfeeling way, to miss the eternal meaning which underlies that image in time, is to perpetrate an outrage which may have disastrous results. On the other hand, such painters as Millet, or even Tissot, in France, as Holman Hunt and Blake, in England, give us a hope that a school of Art may yet arise in which the closing scene of our Lord's life can be effectually treated. What Phidias and Praxiteles did for Zeus or Athene, with perfect success, must be done for the only begotten Son of the Father by men of strong hand and pure heart who have by spiritual assimilation become partakers of His Passion.

The pictures of Tissot could not be obtained for this work from the holders of the copyrights; in some ways they are invaluable, and rich in promise for the future. Under a unique inspiration, received when he was little expecting it, he was driven, as it were, to renounce the world, and devote his whole strength to study and to reproduce the life and death of Jesus. The great crucifix hung high up in the Madeleine, whither he had gone to sketch La Femme à l'orgue, arrested his attention, and, convinced that Christ and His Redemption were the one theme deserving of a life's devotion, he went to Palestine and studied the surroundings of the Lord's life, in order that he might present Jesus to this generation as the first generation saw Him. The success of the consecrated purpose was manifest in that series of drawings which took Paris by storm. But I do not regret that in my part of this volume Tissot's pictures are not included, for in the treatment of the Passion he lamentably failed. In handling the closing scenes of the beautiful Life he could get no inspiration from the scenery or the circumstances of the East. He was thrown back on his fancy to reproduce the Cross and the events which led up to it. Having apparently no inner experience of the Cross, and understanding the Sacrifice only in a sentimental way, he merely exaggerated in endless detail the blood, the torture, the brutality of the situation. And yet this Parisian artist has struck into the path which Holman Hunt, like the earlier painters in Italy and Flanders, attempted to follow. He has reminded the world that to represent the Life of Jesus an artist must live His life, and the suggestion is easily deducible, that to represent the death of Jesus an artist must die with Him.

Robert F. Horton

JESUS CHRIST AT GETHSEMANE.

FROM A PHOTOGRAPH BY HENRY DIXON & SON

John Henry Frederick Bacon, A.R.A.

Elected 1903

THE AGONY IN THE GARDEN. AFTER THE PICTURE IN THE NATIONAL
GALLERY, LONDON, FROM A PHOTOGRAPH BY FRANZ HANFSTAENGL

After Antonio Allegri da Correggio
1494-1534

THE AGONY IN THE GARDEN. AFTER THE PAINTING IN THE BERLIN
GALLERY FROM A PHOTOGRAPH BY FRANZ HANFSTAENGL

Jan Gossaert, known as Mabuse
1470(?)-1541

JESUS CHRIST AT GETHSEMANE: "AND BEING IN AN AGONY HE PRAYED MORE EARNESTLY." AFTER
THE ORIGINAL DRAWING BY PERMISSION OF MISS CASWALL SMITH

Louisa, Marchioness of Waterford
19th Century

From Gethsemane to Olivet

JESUS CHRIST IN THE GARDEN ATTENDED BY AN ANGEL.
FROM AN ORIGINAL PROOF ETCHING

Rembrandt van Rÿn

JESUS CHRIST AT GETHSEMANE.   REPRODUCED FROM A PHOTOGRAVURE BY PERMISSION OF MESSRS.
GOUPIL AND CO.

Charles F. Jalabert
1819-1901

THE KISS OF JUDAS. AFTER THE TEMPERA PAINTING IN FLORENCE IN THE
GALLERY OF ANCIENT AND MODERN ART, FROM A PHOTOGRAPH BY ALINARI

Fra Giovanni Angelico da Fiesole
1387-1455

From Gethsemane to Olivet

JESUS CHRIST TAKEN PRISONER.   AFTER THE TEMPERA PAINTING IN FLORENCE
IN THE GALLERY OF ANCIENT AND MODERN ART, FROM A PHOTOGRAPH BY ALINARI

Fra Giovanni Angelico da Fiesole
1387-1455

THE BETRAYAL OF JESUS CHRIST.   REPRODUCED AFTER THE FRESCO IN FLORENCE IN THE MUSEUM OF
ST. MARK, FROM A PHOTOGRAPH BY ANDERSON, ROME

Fra Giovanni Angelico da Fiesole

1387-1455

FROM GETHSEMANE TO OLIVET

THE REMORSE OF JUDAS.   AFTER THE PICTURE IN THE TATE GALLERY, FROM A PHOTOGRAPH BY
FRANZ HANFSTAENGL

E. Armitage, R.A.
1817-1896

HE REMORSE OF JUDAS   AFTER THE ORIGINAL PICTURE

Albert Goodwin, R.W.S.

THE GOSPELS IN ART

JESUS CHRIST BEFORE CAIAPHAS

PILATE WASHING HIS HANDS

REPRODUCED FROM PRINTS KINDLY LENT BY MESSRS. MAGGS BROTHERS

Albrecht Dürer.

PETER DENIES CHRIST : "THEN SAITH THE DAMSEL THAT KEPT THE DOOR UNTO PETER, ART NOT THOU ALSO ONE OF THIS MAN'S DISCIPLES ?" AFTER THE PAINTING IN THE HERMITAGE, ST. PETERSBURG, FROM A CARBON PRINT BY BRAUN, CLÉMENT AND CO.

Rembrandt van Rÿn
1606-1669

THE GOSPELS IN ART

CHRIST BEFORE PILATE. FROM A PHOTOGRAPH BY BRAUN, CLÉMENT AND CO., BY PERMISSION OF THE OWNER OF THE COPYRIGHT, MONSIEUR CHARLES SEDELMEYER, PARIS

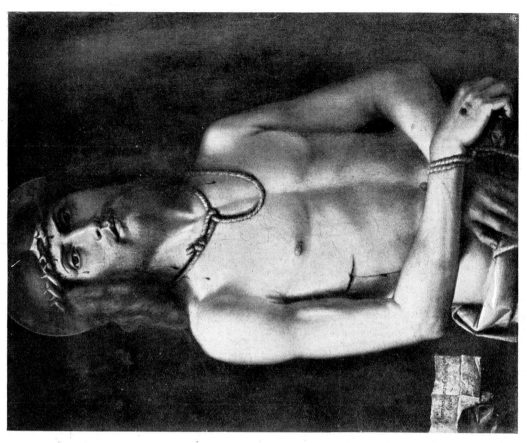

ECCE HOMO. AFTER THE PAINTING IN THE LOUVRE, PARIS, FROM A PHOTOGRAPH
BY M. PERRIER

Bartolommeo Montagna

1450(?)-1523

THE SAVIOUR. AFTER THE DRAWING IN MILAN FROM A PHOTOGRAPH OF
BRAUN, CLÉMENT AND CO., PARIS

Leonard da Vinci

1452-1519

JESUS CHRIST BEFORE PILATE. AFTER THE PAINTING IN THE NATIONAL GALLERY,
LONDON, FROM A PHOTOGRAPH BY FRANZ HANFSTAENGL, MUNICH AND LONDON

Rembrandt van Rÿn

1606-1669

ECCE HOMO.

FROM A PHOTOGRAPH BY ALINARI AFTER THE PICTURE IN THE NATIONAL GALLERY, ROME

Professor Antonio Ciseri

FROM GETHSEMANE TO OLIVET

JESUS CHRIST DERIDED AND INSULTED. AFTER THE TEMPERA PAINTING IN THE ACADEMY
OF FINE ARTS IN FLORENCE, FROM A PHOTOGRAPH BY ALINARI, FLORENCE

Fra Giovanni Angelico da Fiesole

1387-1455

LE CHRIST AU ROSEAU. AFTER THE PICTURE IN THE LOUVRE, PARIS, FROM A CARBON PRINT BY
BRAUN, CLÉMENT AND CO., PARIS

Ary Scheffer

1795-1858

FROM GETHSEMANE TO OLIVET

JESUS CHRIST AT THE COLUMN. AFTER THE CRAYON SKETCH FROM
A PHOTOGRAPH BY BRAUN, CLÉMENT AND CO., PARIS

Jean François Millet
1814-1875

THE GOSPELS IN ART

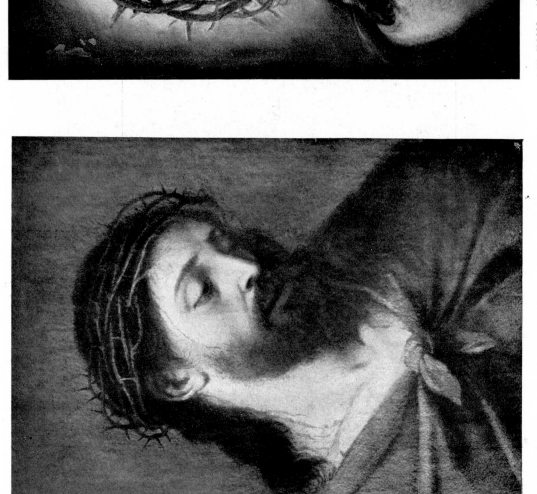

ECCE HOMO.   AFTER THE PAINTING IN MADRID FROM A CARBON PRINT BY
BRAUN, CLÉMENT AND CO., PARIS

ECCE HOMO.   AFTER THE PAINTING IN THE CORSINI GALLERY, ROME, FROM A
PHOTOGRAPH BY BRAUN, CLÉMENT AND CO., PARIS

Guido Reni

JESUS CHRIST AND HIS MOTHER.   AFTER A PHOTOGRAPH BY BRAUN, CLEMENT & CO.

William Adolphe Bouguereau

From Gethsemane to Olivet

HEAD OF JUDAS. AFTER THE FRESCO IN FLORENCE IN THE
CHIESA DI MONTE OLIVETO. FROM A PHOTOGRAPH BY ALINARI

Giovanni Antonio Bazzi (il Sodoma)
1477-1549

JESUS CHRIST AND SIMON OF CYRENE. AFTER THE PAINTING IN THE PINACOTECA COMUNALE AT FORLI,
EMILIA, FROM A PHOTOGRAPH BY ALINARI

Marco Palmezzano
1456 (?)-1538 (?)

THE GOSPELS IN ART

"BUT THE CHIEF PRIESTS MOVED THE PEOPLE THAT HE SHOULD RATHER RELEASE BARABBAS UNTO THEM."
AFTER AN ENGRAVING BY F. LUDY BY PERMISSION OF HENRY GRAVES AND CO.

Friedrich Overbeck
1789-1869

CALVARY.   AFTER THE PAINTING AT VENICE IN THE CHIESA S. ALVISE, FROM A PHOTOGRAPH BY C. NAYA

Giambattista Tiepolo

1696-1770

THE GOSPELS IN ART

THE CRUCIFIXION. AFTER THE PAINTING IN VENICE IN THE CHIESA DI SAN CASSIANO, FROM A PHOTOGRAPH BY ALINARI

Iacopo Robusti (il Tintoretto)

THE CRUCIFIXION. AFTER THE PICTURE AT NAPLES IN THE NATIONAL MUSEUM, FROM A PHOTOGRAPH BY ANDERSON, ROME

Anthony van Dyck

1599-1641

THE CRUCIFIXION. AFTER THE PAINTING IN THE ANTWERP MUSEUM,
FROM A PHOTOGRAPH BY W. A. MANSELL AND CO.

Peter Paul Rubens
1577-1640

THE CRUCIFIXION. AFTER AN ENGRAVING BY PAUL PONTIUS, KINDLY
LENT BY MR. F. B. DANIELL

THE CRUCIFIXION.   REPRODUCED FROM A PHOTO-
GRAPH BY PERMISSION OF FREDERICK HOLLYER,
LONDON

Sir Edward Burne-Jones, Bart.
1833-1898

FROM GETHSEMANE TO OLIVET

HE CRUCIFIXION. AFTER THE ORIGINAL PICTURE FROM A CARBON PRINT BY BRAUN, CLÉMENT AND CC.

Eugène Delacroix
1798-1863

The Gospels in Art

JESUS CHRIST ON THE CROSS.   AFTER THE PAINTING IN THE BELVEDERE,
VIENNA, FROM A CARBON PRINT BY FRANZ HANFSTAENGL

THE DESCENT FROM THE CROSS.   AFTER THE PAINTING IN ST. PETERSBURG,
FROM A PHOTOGRAPH BY FRANZ HANFSTAENGL

Rembrandt van Rÿn

THE DESCENT FROM THE CROSS. AFTER THE PICTURE IN THE
LUXEMBOURG, PARIS, FROM A PHOTOGRAPH BY PERRIER

H. Lazerges
19th Century

THE DEPOSITION FROM THE CROSS. AFTER THE PAINTING IN THE
NATIONAL GALLERY, LONDON, FROM A PHOTOGRAPH BY HANFSTAENGL

Giambattista Tiepolo
1696-1770

THE GOSPELS IN ART

GOLGOTHA—CONSUMMATUM EST. . . . REPRODUCED FROM THE ENGRAVING BY HERMANN EICHENS BY PERMISSION OF MESSRS. GOUPIL AND COMPANY

Jean Léon Gérôme
1824-1904

THE SAVIOUR AFTER HIS PASSION

Francesco Raibolini (il Francia)
1450-1517

THE GOSPELS IN ART

"AND WHEN JOSEPH HAD TAKEN THE BODY, HE WRAPPED IT IN A CLEAN LINEN CLOTH." AFTER THE
PAINTING IN THE LUXEMBOURG, PARIS, FROM A PHOTOGRAPH BY PERRIER

Alphonse Legros

THE BURIAL OF OUR LORD. REPRODUCED FROM AN ENGRAVING BY ALPHONSE LEROY, BY KIND PERMISSION OF MESSRS. GOUPIL AND COMPANY

Charles F. Jalabert

1819-1901

THE GOSPELS IN ART

FROM A PHOTOGRAPH BY EYRE AND SPOTTISWOODE

THE ENTOMBMENT OF JESUS CHRIST

ST. JOHN LEADING THE VIRGIN MARY FROM THE TOMB. FROM A PHOTOGRAPH BY FRANZ HANFSTAENGL, AFTER THE PICTURE IN THE
TATE GALLERY

William Dyce, R.A.
1806-1864

THE RESURRECTION.   AFTER THE PAINTING AT SIENA IN THE PALAZZO DELLA SIGNORIA, FROM A
PHOTOGRAPH BY ALINARI

Giovanni Antonia Bazzi (il Sodoma)

1477-1549

THE HOLY WOMEN AT THE TOMB OF JESUS CHRIST.　　　AFTER A PHOTOGRAPH BY BRAUN, CLÉMENT & CO.

William Adolphe Bouguereau

From Gethsemane to Olivet

Eugène Burnand

"SO THEY RAN BOTH TOGETHER; AND THE OTHER DISCIPLE DID OUTRUN PETER, AND CAME FIRST TO THE SEPULCHRE." AFTER A PHOTOGRAPH OF THE ORIGINAL PICTURE, BY PERMISSION OF MESSRS. BRAUN, CLÉMENT AND CO.

JESUS CHRIST APPEARS TO MARY MAGDALENE. AFTER
THE PAINTING IN THE CORSINI GALLERY, ROME,
FROM A PHOTOGRAPH BY BROGI

Federigo Barocci
1528-1612

JESUS CHRIST APPEARS TO MARY MAGDALENE.
AFTER THE PICTURE IN THE UFFIZI GALLERY,
FROM A PHOTOGRAPH BY ANDERSON

Lorenzo di Credi
1459-1537

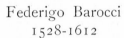

JESUS CHRIST APPEARS TO MARY MAGDALENE. AFTER THE
PICTURE IN THE LOUVRE, PARIS, FROM A PHOTOGRAPH BY
W. A. MANSELL AND CO.

Eustache le Sueur
1617-1655

JESUS CHRIST APPEARS TO MARY MAGDALENE. AFT
PICTURE IN THE NATIONAL GALLERY, LONDON,
PHOTOGRAPH BY W. A. MANSELL AND CO.

Tiziano Vecellio (Titian)
1477-1576

FROM GETHSEMANE TO OLIVET

JESUS CHRIST APPEARING TO THE DISCIPLES ON THEIR WAY TO EMMAUS.   REPRODUCED FROM A
PHOTOGRAPH BY PERMISSION OF MESSRS. BRAUN, CLÉMENT AND CO., PARIS

Eugène Girardet

" PEACE BE UNTO YOU "   FROM A PHOTOGRAPH BY H. DIXON AND SON

John Henry Frederick Bacon, A.R.A.

Elected 1903

LES PÈLERINS D'EMMAÜS : "AND IT CAME TO PASS, AS HE SAT AT MEAT WITH THEM, HE TOOK BREAD, AND BLESSED IT, AND BRAKE, AND GAVE TO THEM." AFTER THE PAINTING IN THE LOUVRE, PARIS, FROM A PHOTOGRAPH BY W. A. MANSELL AND CO.

Rembrandt van Rÿn

1606-1669

THE SUPPER AT EMMAUS. COPYRIGHT 1902 BY BRAUN, CLÉMENT & CO., PARIS. REPRODUCED FROM A PHOTOGRAPH

Eugène Girardet

THE INCREDULITY OF THOMAS.   AFTER THE PAINTING IN THE ANTWERP MUSEUM, FROM A CARBON
PRINT BY BRAUN, CLÉMENT AND CO., PARIS

Peter Paul Rubens

1577-1640

THE GOSPELS IN ART

THE SAVIOUR AFTER HIS RESURRECTION. AFTER THE PAINTING IN THE
PINACOTECA, BRESCIA, FROM A PHOTOGRAPH BY ALINARI

THE SAVIOUR AFTER HIS RESURRECTION. AFTER THE PAINTING IN THE PALAZZO
ROSSO IN GENOA, FROM A PHOTOGRAPH BY BROGI

JESUS CHRIST AFTER HIS RESURRECTION SENDING OUT HIS ELEVEN APOSTLES. FROM A CARBON PRINT BY BRAUN, CLÉMENT AND CO. AFTER THE

CARTOON IN THE SOUTH KENSINGTON MUSEUM

Raffaello Sanzio (Raphael of Urbino)

1483-1520

THE ASCENSION OF JESUS CHRIST. AFTER THE PAINTING IN MUNICH, FROM A PHOTOGRAPH BY
FRANZ HANFSTAENGL

Adriaen van der Werff
1657-1722

HE WAS RECEIVED UP INTO HEAVEN.   FROM A PHOTOGRAPH BY FRANZ HANFSTAENGL AFTER THE PICTURE IN THE
MUNICH GALLERY

Rembrandt van Rÿn

1606-1669

THE APOSTLES IN ART

BEING THE SEVENTH BOOK IN THE ART
AND LIFE LIBRARY AND A COMPANION
VOLUME TO "THE GOSPELS IN ART"
AND "THE OLD TESTAMENT IN ART"

1906

THE ASCENSION.   COPYRIGHT BY THE PHOTOGRAPHISCHE GESELLSCHAFT
BY PERMISSION OF THE BERLIN PHOTOGRAPHIC CO., NEW BOND ST., LONDON

G. Biermann, Modern German School

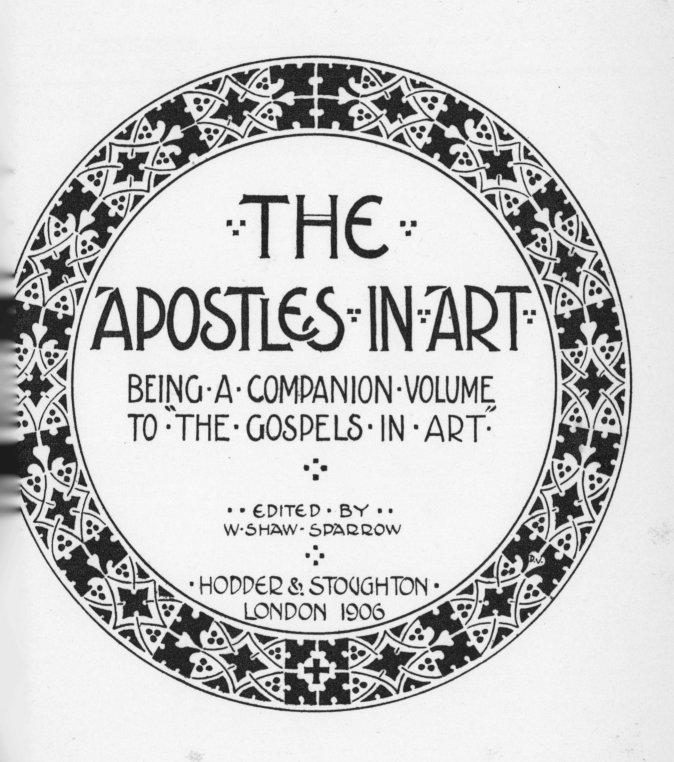

·THE·

·APOSTLES·IN·ART·

BEING·A·COMPANION·VOLUME
TO·"THE·GOSPELS·IN·ART"

··EDITED·BY··
W·SHAW·SPARROW

·HODDER & STOUGHTON·
LONDON 1906

Printed and Bound by
PERCY LUND, HUMPHRIES & CO., LTD.,
The Country Press, Bradford:
And 3, Amen Corner,
London, E.C.

Preface

N attempt is made here, in the present book, to continue the History in Art of the Origins of Christianity. In its own way the subject is as important to us as the Life of Jesus, being the continuation and the complement of that radiant tragedy; and yet, somehow, no book of pictures has been published in our time on the Apostles and their acts. Several reasons for this may be found in the great difficulties which a compiler is called upon to examine and to solve. It is no easy matter to collect good photographs of the scattered pictures, and when they have been collected, the character of the book has still to be considered. A treatment acceptable to experts will be altogether unfriendly to the general public, because most experts are scornful of any but the greatest achievements, while the general public has to rise slowly to the greatest by means of those gently ascending stepping-stones which may be found in the works of the lesser artists. The painters of the world appeal to us ranged in tiers, and to reach the topmost the young student must pass through all the lower tiers or grades.

Again, painters are not usually inspired by the text of any one book; they take their cues from one another, they delight in legends, and they follow the traditions operative in their times; and the result is often perplexing beyond measure to anyone who tries to connect their labours with the supposed origin of their inspiration. The Apostles in Art is a study brimful of incidents of this kind. Indeed, it is as rich on its legendary side as it is in its relation to the Bible text.

In this book the legends are not excluded altogether; they are hinted at here and there; but the main purpose is to illustrate the Acts of the Apostles and the Revelation of St. John the Divine.

It will be noted that the Protestant ideal of St. Paul—the present-day ideal, which culminates with a glowing enthusiasm in the writings of Farrar— has yet to find in art a kindred sympathy and spiritual ardour, a kindred courage and high manliness. Before the Reformation, during the great epochs of encouraged religious painting, St. Paul was not appreciated; and since the Reformation there has been no revival of sacred art which has concerned itself particularly with St. Paul and the Apostles.

W. SHAW SPARROW.

CONTENTS

PHOTOGRAVURE PLATES

MONOCHROME PLATES

THE DESCENT OF THE HOLY GHOST. AFTER THE ORIGINAL PAINTING AT VENICE, IN MADONNA DELLA
SALUTE, FROM A PHOTOGRAPH BY ANDERSON, ROME

Tiziano Vecellio (Titian), Venetian School
1477-1576

General Introduction

By the Rev. R. S. de Courcy Laffan, M.A. Oxon, Rector of St. Stephen's, Walbrook, London, E.C.

N the work here presented to the reader, the period selected for illustration is that which is covered by the Acts of the Apostles, the Epistles of St. Paul, the Catholic Epistles and the Apocalypse. It is, next to the years of Our Lord's ministry, the most momentous period in the history of humanity, for it is the period which witnesses the development of that Divine Society which is to regenerate the world.

At the opening of the "Acts," the Church of Christ is represented by a handful of Galilean peasants, so little awake to the real meaning of their mission that they are still looking for the establishment of a temporal Jewish empire and asking of the Risen Master, "Lord, dost thou at this time restore the Kingdom to Israel?" Before the period closes, the Church has become conscious of itself as a universal spiritual organization for which there is "neither Greek nor Jew, circumcision nor uncircumcision, Barbarian, Scythian, bond nor free:" and it has struck its roots so deep in the great cities of the Mediterranean seaboard that, when the era of persecution dawns under Nero, all the might of the Roman Empire is powerless to eradicate it.

The story of this wondrous inward and outward growth is the story of the Apostles: first of the Twelve, afterwards more especially of St. Paul. But, however clearly we may, and must, recognize the immensity of St. Paul's services to Christianity, we cannot forget that, in the first days of the Church, everything depended on the courage and wisdom of the Twelve. It is justly they who, according to the symbolism of the Apocalypse, have their names inscribed on the twelve foundations of the wall of the City of God, for it was they who laid the first bases of that Kingdom of Christ which has outlasted the seemingly eternal Empire of Rome, and is to endure even to the end of the world.

And if we ask how it came about that this handful of unlearned Galilean peasants were sufficient for these things, the only possible answer is the answer of St. Paul: "their sufficiency was of God." They felt themselves to be in constant touch with that Divine Power and Purpose by which the worlds were

The Apostles in Art

communion with Whom there is kindled in each man's heart the passionate desire for the righteousness which alone can make him worthy of it. All that spiritual development of the idea of God which forms the essential interest of the Old Testament, had been carried on for ages under the forms of a national life. Then the time came when the nation was destroyed by the Babylonian conquest, and the spiritual remnant, disciplined by the experiences of the captivity, was reborn at the Restoration, not as a nation but as a church. United less by the material tie of a common origin, than by the spiritual tie of a common faith, the new Judaism thereby held within itself the potentiality of expansion over all nations, and the dispersion of the Jews, first in the East and later in the West, furnished a multitude of points of contact with the Gentile world, from which that expansion had already begun to radiate, and would radiate with myriad-fold power when once Judaism itself had found the real meaning of its history in the coming of the Christ.

And as in Judæa had been developed by the Divine Providence the passion for righteousness, so in Greece had been developed the passion for knowledge, the intense desire by philosophy, by poetry, by art, to pierce below the shows of things and reach the ultimate realities : to know what the World is and what Man is, what man's place in the world and what his duty in it. That desire, the old hereditary religions were unable to satisfy, neither could it be adequately met by the philosophies beneath whose criticism they were crumbling away. The Greek world, too, was waiting for the revelation of the Christ. Yet the effort of philosophy and literature had not been in vain. By the philosophic discipline of centuries the Greek mind had attained to a power of clear thought which would enable it, when the revelation of Christ came, to recognise in it " the Wisdom of God," and to think it out in its relation to the whole order of the Universe. By the literary discipline of centuries, the Greek language had been wrought into the most perfect instrument which the world has known for the expression of human thought. That Greek thought and Greek language had, first through the colonial expansion of Greece, and afterwards by the con-quests of Alexander, become the common property of the civilized world. When the first preachers of Christianity went forth from Judæa, they were able to speak in one tongue to all the peoples to whom they came. When the books of the New Testament were written in the Greek language they could be read by every educated man of the ancient world.

And yet again, in Rome had been developed through the circumstances of her history the sense of a law and an order ampler and more universal than those

THE DESCENT OF THE HOLY GHOST AT PENTECOST. AFTER THE ORIGINAL PAINTING IN THE MUNICH
GALLERY, FROM A PHOTOGRAPH BY FRANZ HANFSTAENGL, LONDON

Adriaen van der Werff, Dutch School
1659-1722

General Introduction

of any individual nation, while her unique power of assimilating the conquered peoples had familiarized the world with the conception of a human brotherhood transcending all distinctions of race and origin. On the spiritual side, the conquest of the ancient world and the effort of the first Cæsars to weld it into a true civic unity, had created the need for a universal religion which could not be met by the worships of Rome and of the Emperors. On the material side, the establishment of universal peace, and the binding together of the Empire by rapid and secure means of communication, had created a homogeneous medium through which the new thought of Christianity could work with the swiftness and certainty of leaven, while the world-order of the Empire furnished a model for the organization of the Church which was to be co-terminous with the world.

Thus all the centuries of the past had culminated in preparing the way for the reception of the Gospel. Now the moment was come when mankind at large was to be awakened to consciousness of the Divine Purpose which works throughout history. The Apostles had been educated by the Lord of all history in His earthly ministry to be sensitive to every whisper of the will of God. They were now to shape the society which should have for its essential mission to open men's minds to the Divine working in the world, to stir their hearts to co-operate with it, and to arm them with strength from on high that they might co-operate with it victoriously. The shaping of the Divine Society has many stages, only the earliest of which fall within the scope of our present consideration.

In the first days it appears on the small scale of a Jewish community. While it is making its first experiments in the regulation of social life, while its earliest administrative organization is being shaped and its primitive forms of worship are developing, it remains essentially a part of Judaism, " all that believed . . . continuing stedfastly with one accord in the temple," and even the chief Apostles conforming to the temple hours of prayer. The soil of Judaism, saturated with the faith in the One God, the God of Righteousness, was the soil in which the young plant of Christianity, the shoot of Christ's grain of mustard seed, must needs begin its growth. It is in Jerusalem that the first great movement of conversion takes place : it is in Jerusalem that the Church is founded on the rock of St. Peter's stedfastness. Jerusalem is the centre and St. Peter is the leading figure of this first period of the Church's story.

But the Church needs a wider and deeper soil than the hot-bed of Jerusalem can supply, if the grain of mustard seed is to grow into the tree in whose branches the birds of heaven shall come and lodge. Already in the first days, St. Stephen has dimly felt that the forms of Judaism are to pass away, and the thought of

The Apostles in Art

Stephen sinks deep into the soul of Saul the persecutor, soon to become, by his conversion on the road to Damascus, St. Paul the Apostle of the Gentiles. The persecution which arises after the martyrdom of St. Stephen, a persecution providentially restrained until the Church is able to bear it, becomes the direct occasion of the preaching to Gentiles at Antioch, and the formation there of the first Gentile Church. By the divine guidance, St. Barnabas and St. Paul are brought together in the Church of Antioch, and thence are sent by the direction of the Spirit on that first missionary journey to Cyprus, Pisidia and Galatia, by which for the first time the doors of the Church are thrown open to the whole Gentile world. The new movement does not pass without strenuous opposition. Sporadic instances of the admission of Gentile converts had, indeed, already occurred, as in the case of the Ethiopian eunuch and of Cornelius the centurion, but in each case a special revelation had authorized and commanded it. Now the question of general principle is raised, " Can the Gentiles become members of the Church of Christ without also becoming Jews, and being bound to the observance of the whole Jewish law ? " On the decision which shall be given hangs the whole future of Christianity. The Gentile converts have hailed in the coming of the Gospel their deliverance from a religion of forms and outward observances, often beautiful, but incapable of satisfying the yearnings of an earnest soul. They have breathed with joy the larger air of Christianity, they have drunk deep of the spirit of free communion with God and brotherhood with one another. If now they are to be bound down to the keeping of a law of minute rules and childish restrictions, the Gospel will have been preached to them in vain. On the other hand, to the Jew, taught to regard every part of the Mosaic law as divinely and eternally binding, the abrogation of any part of it could not but seem an act of sacrilege. How sharp the contention was, we realize as we read the second chapter of St. Paul's Epistle to the Galatians. Even when the Council of Jerusalem had pronounced authoritatively in favour of liberty, the efforts of the Judaizers to reimpose the observance of the law as a counsel of Christian perfection has still to be met in St. Paul's Letters to the Churches with stern and uncompromising denunciation. But the victory was won, henceforth the preaching of the Gospel was to have free course among the Gentiles.

From this point, St. Paul, the Apostle of the Gentiles, becomes the leading figure in the story of the Church's growth. Through province after province of the Empire, he carries in ever-widening circles the glad tidings of the Gospel : planting the Church in Philippi, in Thessalonica, in Berœa, in Athens, in Corinth, in Ephesus and the cities of the Asiatic province : grouping the new communities on

General Introduction

the model of the provincial organization of the Empire: working out in his letters to the several churches an ever-deepening conception of the Person and work of the Christ. His extraordinary versatility wins him friends in every place and in every rank of society, and enables him to commend the Gospel to men of the most widely different races and degrees of culture: his marvellous activity is unimpaired even by that "thorn in the flesh" which recent investigation has almost conclusively shown to be the recurrence of malarial fever. Neither peril, nor hardship, nor bodily weakness, neither opposition within the Church, nor persecution from without, can hold him back from running the race that is set before him. The authority of the Roman Governor of Achaia, invoked to forbid his preaching, leaves him free to carry the Gospel to any part of the Empire, and before the arrest at Jerusalem closes the story of his missionary journeys as it is told in the Acts of the Apostles, the whole Mediterranean seaboard, from Antioch to Corinth has been studded with Christian Churches which shine "as lights in the world, holding forth the word of life."

In the last chapters of the Acts, the record is the record of "Paul the prisoner of Jesus Christ." The fulness of detail with which these chapters are written enables us to follow step by step the circumstances which, compelling St. Paul to appeal to the High Court of the Empire, bring about the fulfilment of the Master's words, "Be of good cheer, for as thou hast testified concerning me at Jerusalem, so must thou bear witness also at Rome." A series of vivid pictures bring before us all the incidents of the voyage from Cæsarea, the shipwreck, the sojourn at Malta, the arrival in Italy, the first meeting with the Roman Jews. Then the narrative breaks off with the significant words: "And he abode two whole years in his own hired dwelling, and received all that went in unto him, preaching the Kingdom of God, and teaching the things concerning the Lord Jesus Christ with all boldness, *none forbidding him*": the very last phrase of the Acts emphasizing once again the divine providence by which the era of persecution is withheld until the Church is able to bear it.

The story of those two years we piece out for ourselves by means of the letters written from Rome. In the Epistles to the Ephesians, to the Colossians, and to Philemon, we see the Apostle suffering indeed from loss of liberty, but surrounded by faithful friends and in constant correspondence with his converts, watching with anxious care the new problems which are arising in the Church, and led by the danger of the Gnosticism which was beginning to appear in the Churches of Asia, to think out into greater clearness and fulness his doctrine of the Christ and His relation to the whole order of the universe. A little later comes the Epistle to the Philippians, in which St. Paul appears to stand almost alone. In Rome some Christians are even preaching Christ " of envy and strife . . . . . . thinking to raise up affliction for him in his bonds." His friends are for the most part far away. The hour of his trial is at hand. Yet his faith and courage only burn with a clearer flame, and he looks forward confidently to an acquittal which shall set him free once again to start on his missionary travels.

Whether that confidence was justified or not, we cannot say. The last Epistles, those to Timothy and Titus, seem to indicate a short time of liberty followed by a second imprisonment, but it seems impossible to piece them into a coherent narrative. If St. Paul recovered his freedom it was but for a brief space, and the last Epistle to Timothy shows him as having " finished his course," and conscious that " the time of his departure is come."

The era of persecution, long withheld, has dawned at last, and the latest writings of the New Testament show us the Christians everywhere suffering for " the Name."

But the work is done.

Christ's grain of mustard seed has struck root downward, and shot forth upward. Henceforth the wind and the rain of persecution may come. They will but root it more firmly in the hearts of men, they will but inure to greater strength the branches of that tree in which the nations of the earth are to find their habitation.

R. S. DE COURCY LAFFAN.

The Acts, i. to xii.

By the Rev. J. Dobell, Canon of St. Asaph

T the beginning of his story in the Acts of the Apostles, St. Luke makes an interesting reference to his former book, the Gospel. He says that in it he had spoken of all that Jesus "began" both to do and to teach. He suggests to us that he is now going to speak of all that Jesus "continued" both to do and to teach, by the Spirit, by His Apostles, by the faithful disciples.

St. Luke appears to have been a man of Macedonia, probably of Philippi. He, like the rest of the New Testament writers, keeps himself in the background, but occasionally by his use of the word "we," we learn that he himself has a part in the history which he is telling. As he used the word "we" for the first time just after St. Paul had a vision of the man of Macedonia, we may suppose that St. Luke was himself the man of Macedonia whom St. Paul had talked with on the seashore of Troas and whom he afterwards saw in a "vision of the night."

The first chapter of the Acts of the Apostles natur- ally gives us the names of the Apostles, including Matthias, chosen by lot in the place of Judas. It is noticeable that this is the last time in the Bible where anything is decided by lot. Up to this, the casting of lots is a common thing in the Bible. Now, when the Holy Ghost came down to guide the disciples, the decision by lot is no longer needed. Of the Twelve and their future "Acts," we know very little ; of some of them practically nothing at all. But they were the men whose acts and words altered the history of the world, and, as such, they are always honoured in the New Testament. The City of God's building had twelve foundations, the twelve Apostles of the Lamb. Little has been handed down to us concerning them. But we can say of even the least known, St. Matthias, that he "was not nothing because nobody said anything about him."

The Apostles in Art

The Gift of the Holy Ghost was accompanied by the appearance of Divine fire from which a jet of flame rested upon the head of each, by the gift of " other tongues," and by a great sound from heaven which was heard outside in the streets of Jerusalem, causing a multitude quickly to assemble together. Was the gift of " other tongues " a gift of foreign languages ? or was it something still more wonderful ? In Lycaonia, the Apostles seem not to have understood the speech of the people, and our accounts sometimes give us the impression that men of different tongues could understand one speaker. Music is a sort of universal language : men of quite different nationality would understand that a funeral march is a funeral march. Perhaps, amid the wonderfulness of the treasures of God, there may be a speech which, like music, is universal.

In considering the miracles of the Bible, it occurs sometimes to thoughtful minds that perhaps the greatest miracle of all was the change in the character of Simon Peter. Fifty-two days before the coming of the Spirit at Pentecost, Simon Peter was in the court of the palace of the high priest, cursing and blaspheming, asserting angrily that he did not know who Jesus was. And why ? Because he was frightened out of his truthfulness and honesty and loyalty by the pert tongue of a girl at the door. To all appearance a hopeless coward. But on, and after the day of Pentecost, how remarkable was the change. Facing a multitude of perhaps 3000 Jews in the street of Jerusalem, he boldly bears witness to Jesus. " By the hands of lawless men ye did crucify and slay Him." Later (Acts iii.) in the porch of Solomon when " all the people " came together, he testifies " ye asked for a murderer to be granted unto you and ye killed the Prince of life." Again (in Acts iv.) when he is brought before the high priest and his council (the high priest whose maidservant he had trembled before), he speaks undauntedly " in the name of Jesus of Nazareth whom ye crucified," that it cannot " be right in the sight of God to hearken unto you rather than unto God." And before the same council (Acts v.) he with the same courage speaks out for " Jesus whom ye slew. We must obey

The Acts, i. to xii.

God, rather than men." And, when cruelly beaten, he rejoices that he is counted worthy to suffer shame for the Name. Truly the Spirit in a man helpeth his infirmities.

At the end of Acts iv., we have, if a tradition of the early Church can be trusted, an interesting illustration of the truth, "the last shall be first." In our Lord's lifetime, there came to him a rich young ruler, zealous about the keeping of the commandments and anxious to know more about the higher spiritual life. Jesus "beholding him, loved him" and bade him go and sell all that he had and give to the poor. At the time he is quite unequal to such a sacrifice. Joses goes away sorrowful. But the man whom Jesus beheld and loved, cannot go wrong in the end. He did what was required of him at last. "Joses, having land sold it and brought the money and laid it at the Apostles' feet," Joses, who by the name of Barnabas was to come into the very front rank of self-sacrificing workers for God.

In Acts v. we have a striking instance of the special gift of the Holy Ghost, which is called by St. Paul, the "discerning of spirits." St. Peter is thus enabled to distinguish between a true and a false character, between real and sham generosity. A new convert and his wife, Ananias and Sapphira, agree together that they will sell their land and pretend that they are giving the whole price of it to be distributed by the Apostles, while they are really bringing a certain part only. St. Peter not only discerns their deceitful spirit, but sees in the deceit an insult to the "enthusiasm of humanity," then blossoming into flower for the first time in the world. He pronounces their sin to be a lie unto the Holy Ghost and sentences them to a death which is immediately executed by the power of God.

St. Stephen, of whom seven of our pictures tell. Although we only read of him in two chapters, his story is a singularly interesting one. In the three years which followed the day of Pentecost, the Church had greatly increased in numbers. Among the disciples were a large number, not only of Hebrew-speaking Jews who lived in Palestine, but also of foreign Jews who spoke Greek, chiefly from Egypt. There was frequently a

The Apostles in Art

good deal of strife and ill-feeling between these two bodies. And it now threatened to disturb the peace of the Church, the Grecian Jews complaining that in the daily distribution of food, their poor were neglected. As the duties of the twelve Apostles were already sufficiently onerous, it seemed desirable to appoint seven Church officers, "men of good report," to care for the daily distribution. And of these seven, Stephen who was a man full of faith and of the Holy Spirit, quickly took a very prominent part in the defence of the Christian Truth. Men of Alexandria, of Cyrene, and of Cilicia (among whom was doubtless the young Saul of Tarsus) attempted in vain to withstand the wisdom and power of St. Stephen's words. They therefore brought him before the high priest and the council, charging him with blasphemy, craftily weaving into their charge a blending of truth and falsehood. No doubt, he had repeated to them the words of his Master, that " one stone of the temple should not be left upon another." On this they founded an accusation that he had spoken against Moses and against God, against the holy place and the law. St. Stephen's speech in reply is in many ways remarkable. One of those who heard it, Saul of Tarsus, evidently never forgot it. The speech, the death of Stephen, the joy in his face as he had a vision of the Master, his prayerfulness and forgiving spirit as he was murdered, these made a profound impression upon the young mind of Saul. He tried to get away from them, " Kicking against the pricks," till at last he was forced to surrender. And then, as a Christian teacher, he kept again and again reproducing the great lines of St. Stephen's speech as truths which had deeply entered his soul. It is to be noted that in the great speech, St. Stephen made two mistakes. He said that Jacob was buried at Sychem, whereas he was buried at Machpelah ; and also that Abraham bought land of Hamor at Sychem, whereas the purchase was made by Jacob. We have in this a helpful message of encouragement to all earnest workers for God and the truth, bidding them not to be too much afraid of making mistakes. Many a man from shyness, from timidity, from fear of ridicule, not feeling sure that he will escape from making mistakes, hides his one talent

ST. PETER IN PRISON. "PETER THEREFORE WAS KEPT IN PRISON: BUT PRAYER WAS MADE WITHOUT CEASING OF THE CHURCH UNTO GOD FOR HIM." (ACTS XII., 5.) AFTER THE ORIGINAL PAINTING IN THE COLLECTION OF MONSIEUR E. ANDRÉ, FROM A PHOTOGRAPH BY BRAUN, CLÉMENT & CO., PARIS

Rembrandt, Dutch School
1606-1669

The Acts, i. to xii.

in a napkin and buries it in the earth. If St. Stephen had held his eloquent tongue in silence through fear of making a blunder or two, we should have been poorer by the loss of a memorable speech which has helped to alter the history of the world. The adversaries whom he was called to answer, could not believe that "God fulfils himself in many ways" and that it was at least possible that the fulfilment of God's purposes might involve great changes in the future ; they thought that their land would always be the holy land, that their temple would always be the holy place, that their nation must always be thought of as especially the holy nation. In answer to this, he proves to them that God had all along been acting in many varied ways, that there was no Temple before Solomon, that the word of God came to Moses and to Abraham before him, by no means in the Holy Land but in the heathen countries of Midian and Mesopotamia ; and further that their fathers had been, not holy people, but rebellious against Moses, persecutors of the prophets, and full of resistance to the Holy Ghost. Enraged beyond measure, and heedless of justice and fairness, they rise up there and then and murder him. The first martyr, comforted in his agony by a vision of heaven and Jesus at the right hand of God, not seated as we read of Him elsewhere, but standing up to welcome the faithful one to the Home of God, reserved for the true and the brave.

The murder of Stephen and the persecution which followed led to an expansion of the Church's work. Another of the Seven men of good report, St. Philip, has great success in preaching Christ in Samaria and baptizes many, who receive the gift of the Holy Ghost by the laying on of the Apostles' hands. He is then providentially led to encounter the treasurer of Queen Candace, a man of great authority from the neighbourhood of Abyssinia, who may have been the founder afterwards of the early Abyssinian Church. This man had been up to worship at Jerusalem and was returning in his chariot reading the book of Isaiah. Being unable to understand the passage, he is led to ask the help of Philip. He is reading about the "Righteous Servant," who, in captivity in a heathen land, suffered both

The Apostles in Art

from the persecution of the heathens and from the ill treatment of his own renegade countrymen. The captivity was to end not for the sake of the unworthy bulk of the nation, but for the sake of the Righteous Sufferer and those like him who were the salt which saved Israel from corruption. From the thought of that Righteous Sufferer, Philip immediately preaches to him Jesus, Jesus the Prince of all Righteous Sufferers, the fulfilment of all the lives of all true servants of God, who by their patience and agony and death had purchased blessings for their fellowmen ; Jesus who was indeed " led as a lamb to the slaughter; yet He opened not His mouth ; who in His humiliation was robbed of all fair justice and judgment ; and none of His generation considered it, why He was cut off out of the land of the living. For the transgression of His people He was stricken."

After the marvellous conversion of Saul, God gives to His Church a respite from persecution, and the Church has peace. St. Peter goes on a missionary journey to Lydda and Charon and raises up a man named Æneas, who had been paralysed for eight years ; and " all that dwelt there turned to the Lord." In the neighbouring town of Joppa, a still more striking miracle is wrought. A pious woman, Tabitha, Dorcas (the Gazelle) fell sick and died. Her life had been a very valuable one. She had been full of good works and almsdeeds which she did. All the widows had been her care ; she had made for them coats and garments while she was with them. The disciples in their great distress send for Peter. He kneels down and prays by the dead woman ; then giving her his hand, he raises her up ; and, calling the saints and widows, presented her alive.

Our last three pictures refer to the story of the twelfth chapter of Acts. Persecution again rises against the disciples. Herod, to please the Jews, kills St. James, the son of Zebedee, with the sword. He and his brother John had once asked the Lord that He would grant them the places nearest Himself in the kingdom to which He was going at Jerusalem. They little knew that the places they were asking for would prove to be the two crosses of the two thieves on Calvary. Jesus

The Acts, i. to xii.

reminds them that He is going up to be King of Sorrow, Priest of the Worship of Pain, to drink a cup of transcendent bitterness, to be baptized with a baptism of scorching fire. Can they, James and John, join their Master in tasting the bitter cup? Can they too undergo the baptism? With some measure of over-confidence in themselves, but also with some measure of loving loyalty to their King, they reply that they can. And Jesus promises them that so it shall be. To St. James, the promise is fulfilled by his being the first of the Apostles to suffer martyrdom.

" He passed from Herod's flashing blade

" To see Thy Face again "—

St. John's " baptism " is a long life of much pain and patient endurance till he too hears the welcome message, " The Master is come and calleth for thee."

Herod will make yet further concessions to the Jewish rulers. That Easter time is to be memorable in the history of the Church. St. Peter is seized and cast into prison. Four groups of soldiers (four in each group) are to act as " wards " to prevent his escape. There is a group for each of the four watches of the night. The four soldiers are disposed as follows : one outside the prison door, one outside the cell door, and two inside the cell, one chained to either hand of Peter. His case seemed hopeless. His loving friends had only one weapon of deliverance left to them, the weapon of prayer. They could and did pray for him. And God hears and helps. " When thou fearest, God is nearest. The Lord is nigh unto them who are of a broken heart." In the night, an angel comes to rescue Simon Peter. The chains fall from his hands. The cell door lets him through, then the prison door, and then the iron gate of the prison courtyard. Peter, like a man in a dream, cannot believe in his escape till he finds himself alone in the open street in a night lighted up by the passover moon. He makes his way to the house of one of his prayerful friends, Mary, mother of John Mark, and after telling to his amazed and incredulous hearers the story of his being set free, he sends a message to James, the Lord's brother, head of the Jerusalem Church, and then he departed to

The Apostles in Art

" another place," a place well known to the disciples, but not to be described more fully in those days of prosecution.

The measure of Herod's cruelty and wickedness is now nearly full. At Cæsarea, full of arrogance, he accepts as his due the most extravagant adulation and flattery, even allowing with much satisfaction the cries which greet him as a God and not a man. Therefore, because he gave not God the glory, an " angel of the Lord smote him," and, being eaten of worms, he gave up the ghost. It is interesting to read in Josephus also an account of the king's end. He makes no mention of the angel, but states that Herod was seized with violent internal pains and died in five days. Is there not here a clue to much that is often puzzling to us? Josephus and St. Luke tell the same story. But St. Luke, the man of faith, knows of the angel, Josephus knows nothing about him. So, to quote another instance, during the journey of the Israelites through the wilderness, Moses, the man of God, continually saw plain and clear the working of the Hand of an ever-present God; Moses believed and saw. On the other hand, the carnal-minded Israelites did not believe and did not see—their special sin, for which they "entered not in," was unbelief. Doubtless, a modern sceptical writer would have written the Bible stories in a very different way from that of the ancient men of faith. And, on the other hand, the ancient men of faith would write our present history in the light of a constant Divine Presence.

St. Luke in his Gospel told us of all that Jesus began both to do and to teach. In the Book of Acts, he tells us of what Jesus continued both to do and to teach. Jesus, by the pen of St. Luke, has continued to teach us. But He, the Great Teacher, has many things to say to us yet in the coming Eternity, things which pen and ink could hardly write down. May we not hope that when our end draws near, He will say to each : " I have many things to write unto thee, but I would not with paper and ink write them to thee ; but I trust that I shall shortly see thee and that we shall speak face to face."

J. DOBELL.

PENTECOST

THE DESCENT OF THE HOLY GHOST ON THE DAY OF PENTECOST. AFTER AN ORIGINAL MINIATURE
IN A BOOK OF HOURS AT CHANTILLY, FROM A COPYRIGHT PHOTOGRAPH BY GIRAUDON, PARIS

Jean Foucquet, French School
About 1415-towards 1480

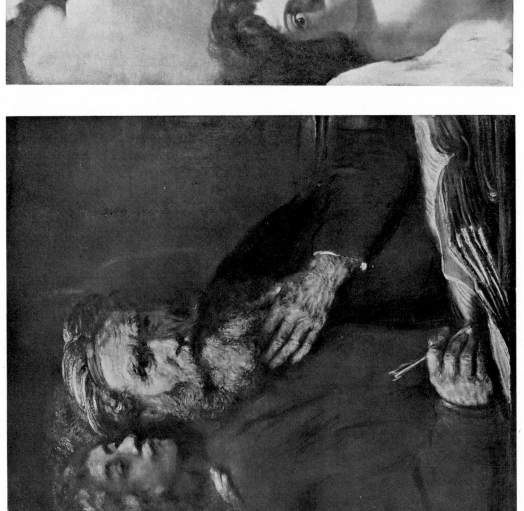

ST. MATTHEW

ST. MATTHEW. AFTER THE ORIGINAL PAINTING IN THE LOUVRE, FROM A PHOTOGRAPH BY NEURDEIN, PARIS

Rembrandt, Dutch School

ST. MATTHEW. AFTER THE PAINTING IN THE DRESDEN GALLERY, FROM A PHOTOGRAPH BY TAMME, DRESDEN

Giov. Francesco Barbieri (il Guercino), Bolognese School

1591-1666

St. Mark and St. Luke

ST. LUKE. IN THE BRERA, MILAN, REPRODUCED FROM A PHOTOGRAPH BY
ANDERSON, ROME

Andrea Mantegna, School of Padua
1431-1506

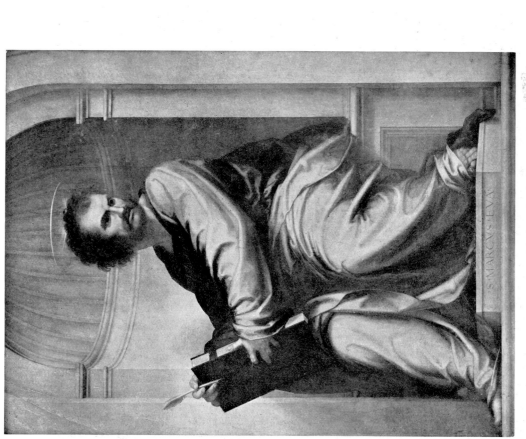

ST. MARK. IN THE PITTI GALLERY, FLORENCE, FROM A PHOTOGRAPH BY
ANDERSON, ROME

Fra Bartolommeo, Florentine School
1475-1517

ST. JOHN AND ST. JUDE

ST. JOHN WRITING HIS GOSPEL. AFTER THE ORIGINAL PICTURE IN THE DRESDEN
GALLERY, FROM A PHOTOGRAPH BY TAMME, DRESDEN

Giov. Francesco Barbieri (il Guercino), Bolognese School
1501-1666

ST. JUDE WITH HIS EMBLEM, THE HALBERD, AFTER THE ORIGINAL PICTURE IN
THE SPENCER COLLECTION, THE PHOTOGRAPH BY HANFSTAENGL, LONDON

Sir Anthony van Dyck, Flemish School

THE APOSTLE ST. JAMES THE GREATER (SANCTUS JACOBUS MAJOR). AFTER THE PAINTING IN THE PRADO
AT MADRID, FROM A PHOTOGRAPH BY BRAUN, CLÉMENT & CO., PARIS

Guido Reni, Bolognese School
1575-1642

THE MADONNA AND MARY MAGDALENE

MARY MAGDALENE, AFTER THE ORIGINAL PICTURE IN THE PITTI GALLERY, FLORENCE, FROM A PHOTOGRAPH BY ANDERSON, ROME

Pietro Vannucci (il Perugino), Umbrian School
1446-1523

THE MADONNA IN PRAYER, AFTER THE ORIGINAL PICTURE IN THE NATIONAL GALLERY, LONDON, THE PHOTOGRAPH BY THE AUTOTYPE CO., 74, NEW OXFORD ST., LONDON

Giovanni Battista Salvi (Sassoferrato), Roman School
1605-1685

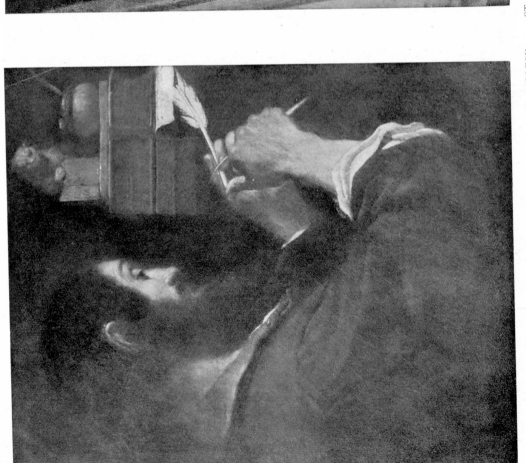

ST. MARK AND ST. LUKE

ST. MARK THE EVANGELIST. AFTER THE PAINTING IN THE DRESDEN GALLERY,
FROM A PHOTOGRAPH BY TAMME, DRESDEN

ST. LUKE THE EVANGELIST. AFTER THE PAINTING IN THE DRESDEN GALLERY, FROM
A PHOTOGRAPH BY TAMME, DRESDEN

Giovanni Francesco Barbieri (il Guercino), Bolognese School
1591-1666

ST. PETER AND ST. BARTHOLOMEW

ST. PETER. AFTER THE ORIGINAL PICTURE IN THE PRADO, MADRID, FROM A
PHOTOGRAPH BY BRAUN, CLÉMENT & CO., PARIS

ST. BARTHOLOMEW. AFTER THE ORIGINAL PICTURE IN MUNICH, FROM A PHOTO-
GRAPH BY F. HANFSTAENGL, LONDON

Josef de Ribera, Spanish School
1588-1656

ST. PETER AND ST. ANDREW

ST. ANDREW THE APOSTLE. AFTER THE PAINTING IN THE PRADO AT MADRID
FROM A PHOTOGRAPH BY ANDERSON

Peter Paul Rubens, Flemish School
1577-1640

ST. PETER. AFTER THE PICTURE IN THE ST. PETERSBURG GALLERY, FROM A
PHOTOGRAPH BY F. HANFSTAENGL, LONDON

Guido Reni, Bolognese School

ST. PETER AND THE APOSTLES RECEIVING CONVERTS INTO THE PRIMITIVE CHURCH AT JERUSALEM.
AFTER AN ORIGINAL MINIATURE AT CHANTILLY, IN THE CONDÉ MUSEUM, FROM A PHOTOGRAPH
BY GIRAUDON, PARIS

Jean Foucquet, French School
About 1415—towards 1480

ST. MATTHIAS. AFTER THE ORIGINAL PICTURE IN THE DRESDEN GALLERY
THE PHOTOGRAPH BY TAMME, DRESDEN

Sir Anthony van Dyck, Flemish School
1599-1641

ST. JAMES THE LESS. A STUDY FOR THE LAST-SUPPER: FROM A DRAWING IN THE
WEIMAR GALLERY, THE PHOTOGRAPH BY BRAUN, CLÉMENT & CO., PARIS

Leonardo da Vinci, Florentine School
1452-1519

St. James the Less and St. Matthias

Sanctus Jacobus Major

ST. JAMES THE GREATER (SANCTUS JACOBUS MAJOR) WITH TWO CHILDREN. AFTER THE
PAINTING AT FLORENCE IN THE UFFIZI GALLERY, FROM A PHOTOGRAPH BY BRAUN
CLÉMENT & CO., PARIS

Andrea del Sarto, Florentine School
1486-1531

ST. PETER

THE PREACHING OF ST. PETER. AFTER THE FRESCO IN
THE CHIESA DEL CARMINE, FLORENCE, THE PHOTOGRAPH
BY ANDERSON

Masaccio, Florentine School
1401-1428
(Sometimes attributed to Masolino, 1383-1447)

ST. PETER IN THE ACT OF PREACHING WHILE ST. MARK TAKES DOWN HIS WORDS IN A BOOK, A PICTURE
IN THE UFFIZI GALLERY REPRESENTING THE TRADITION AS TO THE ORIGIN OF ST. MARK'S GOSPEL. THE
PHOTOGRAPH BY ALINARI

Fra Angelico da Fiesole, Florentine School
1387-1455

ST. PETER AND ST. JOHN

ST. PETER HEALS THE LAME MAN (ACTS III., 4). AFTER
THE ORIGINAL PICTURE IN THE BERLIN GALLERY,
FROM A PHOTOGRAPH BY HANFSTAENGL

Cima da Conegliano, Venetian School
Died about 1517

ST. PETER AND ST. JOHN GIVE ALMS TO THE
POOR. CHIESA DEL CARMINE, FLORENCE, THE
PHOTOGRAPH BY ANDERSON

Masaccio, Florentine School
1401-1428

ST. PETER AND ST. JOHN HEAL THE SICK. AFTER THE ORIGINAL PAINTING IN ST. PETERSBURG, FROM
A PHOTOGRAPH BY FRANZ HANFSTAENGL, LONDON

Joachim Beuckelaer or Beuclaer, Flemish School
1530-1570

PETER AND JOHN HEAL THE LAME MAN AT THE GATE OF THE TEMPLE WHICH IS CALLED BEAUTIFUL.
(ACTS III., 6-7). AFTER THE ORIGINAL CARTOON AT SOUTH KENSINGTON, FROM A PHOTOGRAPH BY THE
AUTOTYPE CO., 74, NEW OXFORD ST., LONDON

Raffaello Sanzio (Raphael of Urbino), Roman School
1483-1520

THE DEATH OF ANANIAS. (ACTS V., 4-5). AFTER THE ORIGINAL CARTOON AT SOUTH KENSINGTON, FROM A
PHOTOGRAPH BY THE AUTOTYPE CO., 74, NEW OXFORD ST., LONDON

Raffaello Sanzio (Raphael of Urbino), Roman School
1483-1520

ST. PETER AND ST. JOHN

A COMPOSITE PICTURE REPRESENTING TWO MIRACLES. ON THE LEFT ST. PETER AND ST. JOHN HEAL THE CRIPPLE AT THE GATE OF THE TEMPLE WHICH IS CALLED BEAUTIFUL. (ACTS III., 7). ON THE RIGHT, ST. PETER AT JOPPA RESTORES TABITHA TO LIFE. AFTER THE FRESCO IN THE CHIESA DEL CARMINE, FLORENCE, FROM A PHOTOGRAPH BY ANDERSON, ROME

Masaccio, Florentine School
1401-1428

(SOMETIMES ATTRIBUTED TO MASOLINO, 1383-1447)

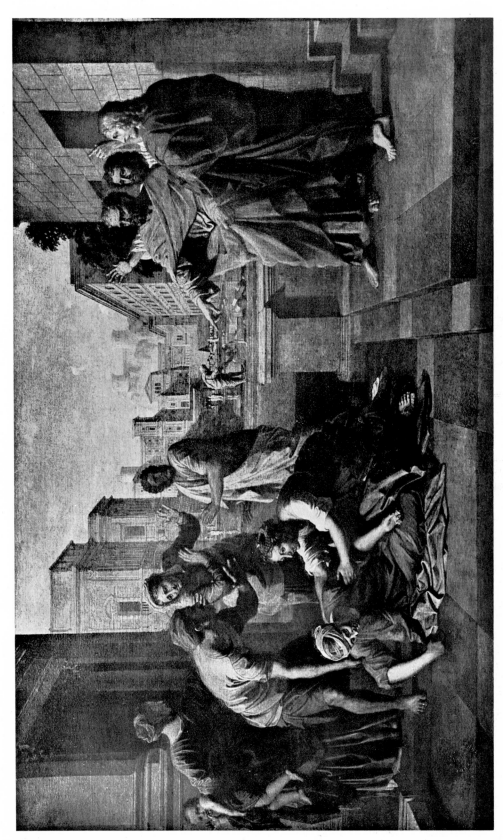

ST. PETER AND SAPPHIRA

Nicolas Poussin, French School
1594-1665

THE DEATH OF SAPPHIRA. "AND PETER ANSWERED UNTO HER, TELL ME WHETHER YE SOLD THE LAND FOR SO MUCH? AND SHE SAID, YEA, FOR SO MUCH. THEN PETER SAID UNTO HER, HOW IS IT THAT YE HAVE AGREED TOGETHER TO TEMPT THE SPIRIT OF THE LORD? BEHOLD, THE FEET OF THEM WHICH HAVE BURIED THY HUSBAND ARE AT THE DOOR, AND SHALL CARRY THEE OUT. THEN FELL SHE DOWN STRAIGHTWAY AT HIS FEET, AND YIELDED UP THE GHOST." (ACTS V., 8-10). AFTER THE PAINTING IN THE LOUVRE FROM A PHOTOGRAPH BY BRAUN, CLÉMENT & CO., PARIS

ST. PETER AND ST. STEPHEN

THE CONFIRMATION OF ST. STEPHEN BY ST. PETER. AFTER THE ORIGINAL PAINTING IN THE BERLIN GALLERY, FROM A PHOTOGRAPH BY BRAUN, CLÉMENT & CO., PARIS

Vittore-Carpaccio, Venetian School
Worked from 1490 to 1519

ST. PETER

THE SICK ARE BROUGHT FORTH INTO THE STREETS, AND LAID ON BEDS AND COUCHES, THAT AT THE
LEAST THE SHADOW OF PETER PASSING BY MAY OVERSHADOW SOME OF THEM. (ACTS V., 15). AFTER THE
ORIGINAL PAINTING IN THE LOUVRE, FROM A PHOTOGRAPH BY BRAUN, CLEMENT & CO., PARIS

Laurent de La Hyre, French School
1606-1656

ST. PHILIP. IN THE UFFIZI GALLERY, FLORENCE, FROM A PHOTOGRAPH BY BRAUN, CLEMENT & CO., PARIS

Albrecht Dürer, German School
1471-1528

St. Stephen

ST. STEPHEN PREACHING TO THE PEOPLE. "AND THE WORD OF GOD INCREASED; AND THE NUMBER OF
THE DISCIPLES MULTIPLIED IN JERUSALEM GREATLY; . . . AND STEPHEN, FULL OF FAITH AND POWER,
DID GREAT WONDERS AND MIRACLES AMONG THE PEOPLE." (ACTS VI., 7-8.) AFTER THE FRESCO IN THE
CAPPELLA DI NICCOLÒ V., VATICAN, FROM A PHOTOGRAPH BY ANDERSON

Fra Angelico da Fiesole, Florentine School
1387-1455

St. Stephen

St. Stephen Preaching. "Then there arose certain of the synagogue, . . . disputing with Stephen, and they were not able to resist the wisdom and the spirit by which he spake." (Acts vi., 9-10.) After the original painting in the Brera at Milan, the photograph by Anderson

Vittore Carpaccio, Venetian School
Worked from 1490-1519

43

ST. STEPHEN PREACHING AT JERUSALEM. "AND THEY WERE NOT ABLE TO RESIST THE WISDOM AND THE SPIRIT BY WHICH HE SPAKE." (ACTS VI., 10.) AFTER THE PAINTING IN THE LOUVRE, FROM A PHOTOGRAPH BY BRAUN, CLEMENT & CO., PARIS

Vittore Carpaccio, Venetian School
Worked from 1490 to 1519

St. Stephen

ST. STEPHEN BEFORE THE HIGH PRIEST. "THEN SAID THE HIGH PRIEST, ARE THESE THINGS SO?" (ACTS VII., 1.) AFTER THE ORIGINAL FRESCO AT ROME IN THE VATICAN, FROM A PHOTOGRAPH BY ANDERSON

Fra Angelico da Fiesole, Florentine School
1387-1455

St. Stephen

ST. STEPHEN ACCUSED OF BLASPHEMY BY THE SANHEDRIN. "'BEHOLD, I SEE THE HEAVENS OPENED, AND THE SON OF MAN STANDING ON THE RIGHT HAND OF GOD.' . . . THEN THEY CRIED WITH A LOUD VOICE, AND STOPPED THEIR EARS, AND RAN UPON HIM WITH ONE ACCORD." (ACTS VII., 56-57). IN THE PRADO, MADRID, THE PHOTOGRAPH BY LÉVY, PARIS

Juan de Juanes, Spanish School
Known also as Vicente Joannes or Vicente Juan Macip
1523-1579

ST. STEPHEN

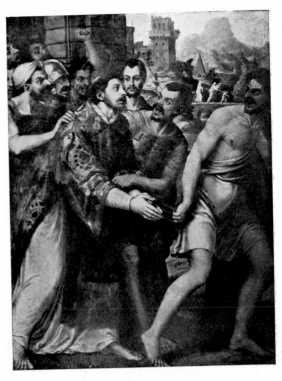

ST. STEPHEN IN THE SYNAGOGUE

ST. STEPHEN LED TO HIS MARTYRDOM

AFTER THE PAINTINGS IN THE PRADO AT MADRID, THE PHOTOGRAPHS BY BRAUN, CLÉMENT & CO., PARIS

Juan de Juanes, Spanish School

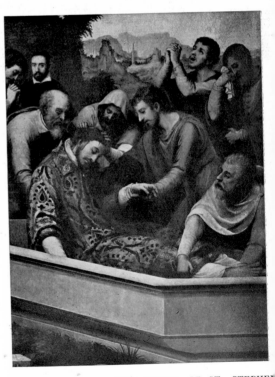

THE BURIAL OF ST. STEPHEN

THE STONING OF ST. STEPHEN

AFTER THE PAINTINGS IN THE PRADO AT MADRID, THE PHOTOGRAPHS BY BRAUN, CLEMENT & CO., PARI

Juan de Juanes, Spanish School
1523-1579

ST. STEPHEN

THE MARTYRDOM OF ST. STEPHEN. AFTER AN ORIGINAL MINIATURE AT CHANTILLY,
IN THE CONDÉ MUSEUM, FROM A PHOTOGRAPH BY GIRAUDON, PARIS

Jean Foucquet, French School
About 1415—towards 1480

St. Peter and St. John

St. Peter and St. John, by prayer and the imposition of hands, give the Holy Ghost to the first converts at Samaria whom Philip the deacon has baptized. (Acts viii., 15-17.) Reproduced from an engraving by permission of Messrs. Henry Graves & Co.

Professor J. Führich, Austrian School
1800-1876

ST. STEPHEN: "HE FELL ASLEEP" (ACTS vii., 60). AFTER THE ORIGINAL PICTURE IN THE TATE
GALLERY, LONDON, FIRST EXHIBITED AT THE ROYAL ACADEMY IN 1895; FROM A PHOTOGRAPH
BY W. A. MANSELL & CO.

Sir John Everett Millais, P.R.A., Modern British School
1829-1896

PHILIP THE DEACON

PHILIP THE DEACON AND THE MAN OF ETHIOPIA, A SERVANT OF GREAT AUTHORITY UNDER CANDACE QUEEN OF THE ETHIOPIANS. "THEN THE SPIRIT SAID UNTO PHILIP, GO NEAR, AND JOIN THYSELF TO THIS CHARIOT. AND PHILIP RAN THITHER TO HIM, AND HEARD HIM READ THE PROPHET ESAIAS, AND SAID, UNDERSTANDEST THOU WHAT THOU READEST?" (ACTS VIII., 29-30.) AFTER THE ORIGINAL DRAWING, DATED 1856, FROM A PHOTOGRAPH BY BRAUN, CLÉMENT & CO., PARIS

R. Julius B. Hubner, German School
1806-1882

ST. PAUL

PAUL'S CONVERSION. AFTER THE TAPESTRY IN THE VATICAN, FROM A PHOTOGRAPH BY ALINARI

Raffaello Sanzio (Raphael of Urbino), Roman School
1483-1520

PAUL'S CONVERSION. AFTER THE ORIGINAL PAINTING AT MUNICH FROM A PHOTOGRAPH BY HANFSTAENGL

Peter Paul Rubens, Flemish School
1577-1640

ST. PAUL AND ANANIAS

ANANIAS AND PAUL. "AND ANANIAS WENT HIS WAY, AND ENTERED INTO THE HOUSE; AND PUTTING HIS HANDS ON HIM SAID, BROTHER SAUL, THE LORD, EVEN JESUS, THAT APPEARED UNTO THEE IN THE WAY AS THOU CAMEST, HATH SENT ME, THAT THOU MIGHTEST RECEIVE THY SIGHT, AND BE FILLED WITH THE HOLY GHOST." (ACTS IX., 17)

Jean Restout, French School
1692-1768

ST. PAUL ESCAPES FROM DAMASCUS. "THEN THE DISCIPLES TOOK HIM BY NIGHT, AND LET
HIM DOWN BY THE WALL IN A BASKET." (ACTS IX., 25)

Reginald Hallward, Modern British School

THE CHARITY OF DORCAS. "NOW THERE WAS AT JOPPA A CERTAIN DISCIPLE NAMED TABITHA, WHICH BY
INTERPRETATION IS CALLED DORCAS: THIS WOMAN WAS FULL OF GOOD WORKS AND ALMSDEEDS WHICH SHE
DID." (ACTS IX., 36.) REPRODUCED BY PERMISSION OF HENRY GRAVES & CO.

W. C. T. Dobson, R.A., Modern British School
1817-1898

St. Peter

ST. PETER HAVING RESTORED TABITHA TO LIFE PRESENTS HER TO THE SAINTS AND WIDOWS. (ACTS IX., 41.)
AFTER THE ORIGINAL PAINTING IN THE LOUVRE, FROM A PHOTOGRAPH BY BRAUN, CLÉMENT & CO., PARIS

Pierre Jacques Cazes, French School
1676-1754

ST. JAMES THE GREATER

THE MARTYRDOM OF ST. JAMES THE GREATER (SANCTUS JACOBUS MAJOR), THE SON OF
ZEBEDEE AND THE BROTHER OF JOHN. (ACTS XII., 1-2.) AFTER THE ORIGINAL MINIATURE
IN A BOOK OF HOURS AT CHANTILLY, THE PHOTOGRAPH BY GIRAUDON, PARIS

Jean Foucquet, French School
About 1415—towards 1480

ST. JAMES THE GREATER AND ST. JAMES THE LESS

ST. JAMES LED TO EXECUTION. AFTER THE PAINTING AT
PADUA IN THE CHIESA DEGLI EREMITANI, THE PHOTOGRAPH
BY ANDERSON, ROME

Andrea Mantegna, School of Padua

MES THE GREATER. BROTHER OF JOHN, CONDEMNED TO
BY HEROD AGRIPPA. "NOW ABOUT THAT TIME HEROD
NG STRETCHED FORTH HIS HAND TO VEX CERTAIN OF
HURCH. AND HE KILLED JAMES THE BROTHER OF JOHN
WITH THE SWORD." (ACTS XII., 1-2.)

THE MARTYRDOM OF ST. JAMES THE LESS, BROTHER OF THE
LORD, WHOM TRADITION REPRESENTS AS BEING SLAIN WITH
A FULLER'S CLUB OR HAMMER. AFTER THE ORIGINAL PAINTING
AT PAUDA, IN THE CHIESA DEGLI EREMITANI, THE PHOTO-
GRAPH BY ANDERSON, ROME

Andrea Mantegna, School of Padua, Venetia
1431-1506

St. Peter

ST. PETER IN PRISON IS AWAKENED BY THE ANGEL. AFTER THE ORIGINAL PAINTING IN ROME, FROM
A PHOTOGRAPH BY BRAUN, CLÉMENT & CO., PARIS

Domenico Zampieri (il Domenichino), Bolognese School
1581-1641

ST. PETER DELIVERED FROM PRISON. "AND THE ANGEL SAID UNTO HIM, GIRD THYSELF, AND BIND ON THY SANDALS. AND SO HE DID. AND HE SAITH UNTO HIM, CAST THY GARMENT ABOUT THEE, AND FOLLOW ME. AND HE WENT OUT, AND FOLLOWED HIM; AND WIST NOT THAT IT WAS TRUE WHICH WAS DONE BY THE ANGEL; BUT THOUGHT HE SAW A VISION." (ACTS XII., 8-9.) IN THE VATICAN, ROME, FROM A PHOTOGRAPH BY ANDERSON

Raffaello Sanzio (Raphael of Urbino), Roman School

1483-1520

The Pauline Period

By the Rev. R. C. Gillie, M.A.

I. THE APOSTLE PAUL, HIS PERSONALITY.

IT is difficult to overestimate the service St. Paul rendered to Christianity. To this day it is realized in an imperfect fashion by a large section of Christendom. He found the Church a Jewish sect. He left Christianity a world-wide religion. So long as the teaching of Jesus was regarded as an 'adjunct of Judaism, grafted on to the old stem of the Law, it could never become a universal religion, however tenderly and mystically understood by its expounders. It would have remained a creed rejected by the Jews as a nation, and so closed against the Gentiles by the narrow gates of Judaism through which they would have to pass, that the idea of universalism which lay behind the life and teaching of Jesus could never have come to realization. Through St. Paul the bonds were burst. When he died, the gates were wide open, welcoming all men.

All his youth had been spent in enthusiastic reverence for the Law. He had sat at the feet of Gamaliel, that great spiritual minded Jew, whom a French writer of Palestinian romance has pictured as finally acknowledging Christ. Burning with zeal for his hereditary faith, he had come up to Jerusalem from Tarsus, to be instantly filled with anger and disgust at the new doctrines which day by day sickened his ears. Yet Saul, the persecutor, must already have had implanted within him some seeds of dissatisfaction with the old way. His nature yearned for perfection. The fulfilling of the Law was the only road he could recognise—a law which hedged his life within a moral code and filled every hour with wearisome minutiæ of duty, which robbed his soul of all spontaneity, and which, moreover, he could never fulfil. If he failed and the burden of his failure became intolerable, what of the others? What hope for the little people of the nation, living from hand to mouth, less educated, with less leisure, in every way with less chance ? Still, if it were the only way, it must be pursued. With the burden of failure growing always heavier, he must go on, knowing that in their imperfection he and his people must stand finally condemned before God. His ever sensitive conscience would not suffer him to be blinded with the subterfuges which comforted meaner natures. The will of God had been made known through the Law once and for all until such time as the Messiah, no criminal to die miserably on a gibbet, but the King, representative of Jehovah, should come to strengthen the faithful. A feeling of miserable necessity drove the sincere soul forward. Not the transfigured beauty of dying Stephen could change his course.

Through this same man, while he hurried to bear a fuller part in the extermination of the followers of Jesus, God set His seal to the liberty of His human children. Saul, afire for holiness yet burdened with a burden no man could carry, had his wayside vision—a vision of reproach but of such blessed meaning, that the reproach is swallowed up in joy. Jesus, speaking from Paradise, was no criminal, but the great Son of God. The old way of heartbreaking hardness which only seemed to urge a man to sin, was not the path men were called to tread. Saul blind, alone, helpless, now regarded with enmity by the Jews both of the old and of the new order of things, smitten with sorrow for his failure to recognise the footsteps of his Lord, is yet moved with a very convulsion of joy. From that moment he received into his soul the Lord himself. Henceforward he is dead to an external law. From within flows the love which is the fulfilling of all law. He is the child of God, wrapped round by His mercy, assured that error, failure and sin are alike blotted out in Divine forgiveness.

There is but scanty history of the ten intervening years, before he began his life work. Probably they were spent for the most part in Tarsus, working at his trade, growing into silent realization of the new truth, tentatively testing his power to proclaim it. We hear of a solitary sojourn in the deserts of

The Pauline Period

Arabia, where in silent self-communings, he became more and more sure of the great work wrought in him. The historian is right to pass rapidly over this period. It was not a time of creation but of maturing. He dwells upon the pivotal moment of experience. At Damascus, Saul the prisoner of the Law died, and in his place came Paul, the prisoner of Christ, the apostle of the Gentiles, unfaltering in his mission. One great fact he had grasped. The way was not merely Jewish, a new development of the old order. It was a revelation of God to the whole world, which if a man should accept, demanded neither circumcision nor temple ceremonial. It meant nothing less than the indwelling of Christ for all who would receive Him; it was the high liberty and beloved bondage of the believer.

As soon as the clear call to become the herald of the Christ was heard, Paul, the apostle of God, not of men, concentrated himself upon his vast task. His first missionary journey in which he was perhaps limited as much as strengthened by his companion Barnabas, was but a preliminary experiment. Soon we see him hastening with unflagging zeal over land and sea, to win converts for his Master. With consummate strategy he follows the great roads, omits the smaller towns and the villages, and hurls himself on the citadels of ignorance and vice in the chief places of population. With equally skilful tactics, he begins in every place in the synagogues of the Jews, where he knows there must be some with a past experience like his own, eager for an enlightenment like his. From this vantage ground he approaches the true seekers among the Gentiles, and with mingled ardour and ingenuity, " made himself all things to all men that by all means he might save some." Both his plan and the success which attended it are of world-historic importance. " It is a great deal more than a mere fanciful comparison when it is said that the apostle's great missionary journeys from Antioch to Rome were a repetition of Alexander the Great's conquests, only in the opposite direction."

Nor did the apostle's eager advance make him neglectful of the positions already won. Though foremost in

The Apostles in Art

the vanguard, in daily hand-to-hand conflict with the votaries of the gods of Greece and Rome, he has an eye for every corner of the battlefield. His epistles are not theological treatises, composed in studious calm. With hardly an exception they are drawn from him by the exigencies of some little community of believers, whom he has captured and has left behind like a little *colonia* of the city of Heaven in the midst of hostile forces. Hence the strange mingling in these letters of doctrinal statement, of moral exhortation, and of friendly greeting and appeal. He is prodigal of effort to maintain what he has won for Christ. He will not allow himself to neglect a single detail of conduct, nor does he leave any worthy expedient of conciliation untried. When in imminent danger of death at Ephesus and racked by the news of the insubordination and licentiousness of the Corinthian Church, he exerted himself in the collection of alms for the poor Jewish Christians of Jerusalem. His devotion to his work knows no bounds. He could wish himself accursed that his nation might be saved. He outrages his humility that he may move the Corinthians by the catalogue of his sufferings and overawe them by the recital of his most private spiritual privileges. The lapse of a single convert profoundly affects him. "Who is weak and I am not weak? Who is made to stumble and I burn not?" he cries. Like Cæsar and Napoleon, he apparently suffered from nervous disorders, serious enough to have made some men play the role of semi-invalids. Like these great generals, he is filled with a world-conquering ambition, but it is the ambition to make all men the happy slaves of Jesus Christ.

There is only one poem—it might almost be said, only one work of art—which has presented to the modern mind the intensity, the well-nigh intolerable urgency of this herald of Christ. In the rushing rhythm and alliterative poise of F. W. H. Myers' poem, "St. Paul," the impetuous but mastered energy of the apostle is recalled by the form as well as the thought of the lines. Almost any selection glows with the fire of his illimitable love for Christ. The following stanzas present him in his most characteristic attitude of appeal:

ST. PAUL AND ST. MARK. AFTER THE PAINTING IN
THE MUNICH GALLERY, THE PHOTOGRAPH BY
F. HANFSTAENGL

Albrecht Dürer, German School
1471-1528

The Pauline Period

Oh could I tell, ye surely would believe it !
  Oh could I only say what I have seen !
How should I tell or how can ye receive it,
  How, till He bringeth you where I have been ?

Therefore, O Lord, I will not fail nor falter,
  Nay but I ask it, nay but I desire,
Lay on my lips thine embers of the altar,
  Seal with the sting and furnish with the fire ;

Give me a voice, a cry and a complaining—
  Oh let my sound be stormy on their ears !
Throat that would shout but cannot stay for straining,
  Eyes that would weep but cannot wait for tears.

Quick in a moment, infinite for ever,
  Send an arousal better than I pray,
Give me a grace upon the faint endeavour,
  Souls for my hire and Pentecost to-day !

Seeing that the Church owed so much to the apostle, and was transformed chiefly by his agency from a provincial influence to a world power, it is scarcely surprising that some should be inclined to exaggerate his importance. Just because a large section of Christendom had failed to realize the vital part he had played in formulating the Christian religion for the world, there was a temptation to press to the other extreme. A number of writers have contended that he must occupy a higher place than Jesus, as he was the decisive factor in the development of the Faith. While this misconception appeals to us as quaint rather than blasphemous, it has been put forward with sufficient force to dispose us to pause before it. Its failure to understand Paul is as conspicuous as its failure to honour Jesus.

That Paul was a man of quite extraordinary individuality is certain, and it is therefore the more remarkable that his every fibre was consciously dominated by Christ. He became so filled with the sense of His dominion that even while his intensity was redoubled by this new force within him, he was aware of a kind of personal obliteration. He uses the strongest expressions in declaring his dependence upon his Lord. The " slave of Jesus," the " prisoner of Jesus," " crucified with Christ,"—he hesitates at no metaphor to convey this idea. And this dispossession of his own personality by the presence of Jesus continues right to the end. It bears the test of five and twenty years of hardship and spiritual trial.

It may be suggested that examples are to be found of great natures dominated by men of meaner quality and less ability. Laurence Oliphant, the distinguished author of more than one original book, was completely dominated by the man Harris, who would not be remembered at all upon his own merits. But this instance confutes the contention. He who is truly the source of inspiration maintains his high place to the end. Harris dwindled not only in general estimation, but in that of his most eminent disciple, who finally broke with him. Such a case only proves the futility of such comparisons. With Paul, we see the continually rising flood of his passion for Christ. It is the mark of the saints, the proof of the indwelling of the Master, which they urge upon us. Paul with his unimpressive person, his recurring illness, his almost harsh enthusiasms radiates something of the very nature of Christ, and in spite of his unmeasured condemnations of his antagonists, has " so learned Christ " as to rank love as the very essence of God. This is the determinant consideration. Paul drew the life blood of his soul from Jesus. Jesus had no need to derive from any man.

In turning the pages of the Evangel, we receive an impression of wonderful unity. Here is a life written by four men of varying character and temperament, and at any point upon which we may seize the effect upon us is one of utter nobility and greatness—something so unique that it is impossible to turn away either indifferent or repelled. We are in contact with a supreme Spirit, before whom we unconsciously lower our own opinions. We may in the end reject Him, because the standard urged on us is too high, because our love of this world is too great, because we feel He will tend to quench our material joys—never because we find anything unbeautiful, insignificant, or disproportionate. Even Nietzsche, apparently only willing to know Christianity through the medium of a narrow theology and filled with passionate rancour against Christian ideals, gives

The Pauline Period

his egoism pause before this august Figure. " He was noble enough "—one feels is an expression forced from him against his will.

It is quite otherwise with St. Paul. It is possible to imagine one ignorant of his story, opening the epistles at random and turning away indifferent or even repelled. In his vigorous denunciations, while never the fruit of personal rancour, we sometimes miss the ring of outraged love which marks those of the gospels. His vehemence may flash out upon us with something unbeautiful and harsh. His conception of marriage in the Epistle to the Corinthians would strike the casual reader as less than logical and even a little ignoble. These defects are just in short the tokens of his humanity where he is not entirely possessed or directed by Christ. Here is the last remnant of the Pharisee who was once a bigot, of the man who had it in him to persecute a little hunted community of enthusiasts for the glory of God— it is the fading trace of the chief of sinners whom he sadly arraigns before his own conscience.

To love Paul, then, there must be no desultory reading. We are not immediately enchained. We must know his history, understand the convulsion which gripped and changed his life, understand his love for his friends, his almost fierce but always beautiful exaltations, the limitations imposed by his physical frame, his subtle metaphysical genius, and, above all, we must realize the central fire which consumed his baser self so that he is unendingly ready to part with old prejudices and preferences, only longing for the coming of the kingdom. To those who accept, like the present writer, the epistle to the Ephesians as genuinely Pauline, it is clear that his old ideas on marriage, which seem to us less than beautiful, are swept away with fuller experience of Christ, and marriage is raised to be a symbol of nothing less than the union of Christ with His church. In this epistle, as in the Epistle to the Philippians, we find Paul completely impregnated with the new ideals of the relation of God to His children, which he has received from his Master. The apostle owed the consummation of his character and the flowering of his religious genius, as entirely as his conversion, to none other than Jesus.

It is true that Paul, more than any other, was the means of making Christianity the world-wide religion it has become, affecting even the nations which do not acknowledge its sovereignty. He planted and organized churches, he taught them, watched over them, rebuked them, loved them, but an organization of the most perfect kind could scarcely have held together, much less advanced, without the vital spark from a higher source. He was the means, the human instrument, the creature used by God, but he was ever ready to abase himself before Christ, who was to this man with his intellectual subtlety, his splendid conscience and his belief in moral beauty, the great loveliness without flaw.

To those who know the incomparable heroism of St. Paul, above all to those who have been able to enter into his exquisite mysticism and thus have avoided the double error of underestimating or exaggerating his influence, there remains an almost insoluble riddle. Why, when he did so much for the founding and organizing of the Church, did he receive so little honour at the Church's hands ? St. Polycarp declared, "Neither am I, nor is any other like unto me, able to follow the wisdom of the blessed and glorious Paul." But how soon the Church of the early centuries ceased to give him a foremost place. Again, at the Reformation, when warm personal feeling at length awoke, why was this affection for him so short-lived ? For light, for leading, for support, the rulers in the Church referred to him continually, yet it would seem that he has been continually dwarfed by some other saint. One can understand the precedence given to the companions of our Lord, particularly to St. John, who was the friend as well as the disciple, and who is the arch-mystic in the Christian Calendar. In the Roman Church, St. Peter, of course, overshadows him entirely. But it is surprising that he has not received in that church the adoration given to lesser men. St. Joseph, St. Anthony, St. Aloysius, and many others have their shrines and their following. "St. Paul has always remained a stranger to the soul of the people." One

The Pauline Period

has a sense of gratitude in the church of St. Peter and St. Paul at Venice, and in San Paolo fuori le Mura at Rome, where at least, as so rarely in other cities, he is given a high place. Our own metropolitan church is another splendid exception.

As a matter of fact, the apostle was and still is a point of conflict. He may be termed the first Protestant, yet the latest German commentator upon his ideas, in a volume of great force and brightness, declares that the apostle stands in part for both Catholicism and Protestantism. In like manner other strange dislocations of opinion may be traced to his influence. He is a paradox. His soul was a battlefield. His life was one long campaign. His missionary career was a dire struggle with the alien ideas and moralities of Gentile peoples, and with the crippling ceremonialism and religious bondage of his own nation. His own inner experience had seen a conflict of the most intense kind, which has been burned into the heart of humanity by the vii. chapter of the Epistle to the Romans. Uncertain physical strength caused him to be unceasingly fighting with the failing flesh, clamant for repose. Thus his personality has emerged upon us with some elements of unrest and battle which have never forsaken it. His epistles have been studied as the invaluable armouries of controversial theology, and as the sublimest treatises on Divine loving kindness, while the man himself has been left unshrined and scarcely loved. It is as though through a glorious and unconscious abnegation of spirit, he had made it impossible for the world to remember him even by its gratitude.

II. ST. PAUL IN ART.

When we come to consider the portrayal of Paul in art we are at once struck with the same curious incompleteness of appreciation which we have met with in the Church. In the first place, he is not so frequently depicted as the important part he had played would seem to warrant; and secondly, even when the centre of a really noble group executed with some imagination and power, his is the one figure which rarely carries conviction. There are two reasons which account to a large extent for this. No doubt the strong tradition which had been handed down from the earliest centuries of his personal insignificance decided many painters against taking him as their subject at all. It was said that he was small, crooked, diseased. One account went so far as to specify a hideous disease of the eyes which made him repulsive to look upon—a tradition which Professor Ramsay has dissipated by pointing out the frequent references to his " fixed gaze," leading one to suppose that the power of his eyes over the person he was addressing was a marked trait.

And if all this in part accounts for the infrequency of pictures representing him, there is no doubt that those painters who attempted the task often fail to impress us from want of clearness in their own mental vision. There are many exquisite St. Johns all approximating more or less to a fixed type; for St. John, beautiful and mystically devotional, had assumed clear and exquisite outlines to men's minds. St. Peter, too, we generally find vigorously delineated, and the Baptist full of strenuous appeal. With St. Paul it is usually quite otherwise. He was too many-sided and too inadequately understood ever to have taken definite shape in the popular mind. There was at once something elusive and perplexing about a man who had shown so many aspects to the world, who was so versatile and subtle a thinker and so impetuous a leader. And thus it comes about that those painters who have laid aside the unattractive tradition of his person have for the most part created a merely massive and dignified Father in the Church, giving no indication of the distinction and ardour of spirit of which he was possessed.

It is quite certain that a history of Paul, as he figured in men's thoughts through the centuries during which he has been at least partially read and studied, would show us very considerable changes and fluctuations which are reflected in the works of the artists. The Catholic Church, while she was in the main the result of the labours of the Apostle to the Gentiles, was apt to overlook her debt in her devotion to Peter, and having drawn but little from the Pauline epistles, has appeared to shut away the author from us by the rigidity of her dogmatic theology.

The Pauline Period

It is indeed as though Paul, about whom there was nothing rigid whatever, but whose spirit had all that flexibility which accompanies continual growth, was to suffer even after his martyrdom not one imprisonment, but several. The mediæval church, looking upon him as one who had helped to establish the supremacy of Rome, linked him with Peter, suggesting thereby a kinship of spirit between two men who really differed entirely in impulse and intellectual outlook, and whose one common bond was devotion to Christ. This misconception bore fruit later in many renaissance pictures which represented him as in some sort a second Peter, but of infinitely less character. The real Paul was effectually hidden by a priesthood which more and more taught salvation by works, and which had elaborated such doctrines as works of supererogation and indulgences. Besides, many legends, quite without historical basis, had been eagerly cherished because connecting St. Peter and St. Paul with Rome. Such were the accounts of the competition for mastery with Simon Magus, and such the detailed stories of their martyrdoms. All this played its part in obscuring the real Paul, for in the Pauline legend there was little of the tender play of imagination which lent poetic value to many apocryphal stories concerning Christ, and to a few concerning Peter. Certainly nothing is found to equal the beauty of the story which led to the building of the Church of *Domine quo vadis* at the entrance to the Appian way.

But the great spirit of Paul was not always to be withheld from the Christian world. The stress and struggle of the Reformation burst the prison doors the church had closed upon him, and once more his doctrine of pardon and freedom through justification by faith was to be a centre of thought and belief. It was as though the apostle himself had emerged to the contest, for those wonderful letters, retained by the church and in theory regarded and reverenced, were once more to play a vital part in breaking the cruel bondage of the law which had been his own despair. But if Luther and Calvin had restored Paul to his place, dogmatic Protestantism was to undo much of their work. As doctrine and thought hardened into set forms, the passion and poetry disappeared, and the letters that had filled men with religious enthusiasm came to be regarded and used very much as legal documents. Still the Reformation did produce its painter before the light of its great day had faded, and Dürer has given us noble pictures of the apostles, amongst which is a notable St. Paul.

We find in this collection six painters at least who have made a distinct attempt to give us Paul the man. Only two of them are of the same nationality, and they use widely differing methods. They are Dürer, Rembrandt, Masaccio, Guido Reni, Alonso Cano, and one modern painter, Frederic Shields.

To the picture by Dürer I have already alluded. It possesses added importance, because considered by some, who have devoted themselves to the subject, to be the finest and most individual picture of Paul in existence (p. 60). It makes an immediate impression of unusual strength of character combined with subtlety and alertness, and, moreover, helps us to understand the vehemence with which this man was either loved or hated. Indifference would be impossible, any feeling he inspired must have been intense. He is represented without a suggestion of physical disability. His tenacity and clearness of vision are matched by the powers of endurance indicated by his physique; he is pre-eminently a leader. He has not, perhaps, the sensitiveness of the real Paul, but that the poet should be less prominent than the man of action has more than an element of truth, for the poetry that bursts forth in the epistles, while it is of the highest order, has the heroic quality of being the spontaneous outcome of his ideas and devotion.

In the Rembrandt, a picture of superb power, we find a representation quite as remarkable though differing in many essentials (p. 74). The lined, rugged, old face glowing out of the shadows is surely as fine as any that great master has given us, and is absolutely arresting in its strength and individuality. Yet this is hardly the man who hurried urgently from city to city, unresting and homeless, consumed with a passion for the conquest of the world for his master Christ. This is rather a kindred soul

ST. PAUL AT ATHENS. "THEN CERTAIN PHILOSOPHERS OF THE EPICUREANS, AND OF THE STOICKS, ENCOUNTERED HIM. AND SOME SAID, WHAT WILL THIS BABBLER SAY? OTHER SOME, HE SEEMETH TO BE A SETTER FORTH OF STRANGE GODS: BECAUSE HE PREACHED UNTO THEM JESUS, AND THE RESURRECTION." (ACTS XVII., 18). AFTER AN ORIGINAL DRAWING FROM A PHOTOGRAPH BY BRAUN, CLEMENT & CO.

Alexandre Bida, Modern French School
1808-1895

The Pauline Period

than the apostle himself; equally strenuous and urgent in thought and a great controversialist, but a man of books, happiest in his library, and with his manuscripts. His kinship lies more in an eagerness of soul which the years cannot cloud, than in any other trait. He is magnificent, untiring, the student who thinks passionately—and in all this, is truly Pauline; but there is a shadow here which never rested upon the spirit of Paul—the shadow of a troubled questioning, I had almost said of struggling faith.

The third St. Paul, undoubtedly to be reckoned with these in greatness, is of an earlier date, and is to be found in the fresco in the Brancacci Chapel in the Carmine in Florence, which Masaccio is said to have left unfinished at the time of his mysterious disappearance in 1428. Many years later, this fresco, which represents the apocryphal incident of the king's son being raised from the dead, was very nobly completed by Filippino Lippi. The apostle kneels beside the youth, his hands joined in prayer, his face upraised, and his eyes beholding no bystander but some vision of the soul. He is the man of a single burning purpose by whom suffering and disease are hardly remembered, save as a hindrance to the carrying of his message, and who reckons persecution all joy for the sake of Christ. The dark, vivid face with its passionate tenacity, would be that of a fanatic but for its suggestion of thought and balance. This is perhaps more really the man than any other (p. 92).

From these three masterpieces we make a great descent when we pass on to Guido Reni and Alonso Cano. Guido Reni had a great reputation in that dark day which saw the entire neglect of the glories of Botticelli, and in Hawthorne's "Transformation" we find him ranked with the Titans. As a matter of fact he had much of the grandiose method and shallowness of thought of the eclectic school, and it is one of the riddles of painting how he ever came to produce work of such lasting charm as the so-called Beatrice Cenci of the Palazzo Barbarini, and the glowing ceiling painting of Phœbus and Aurora in the Palazzo Rospiglosi. He was the forerunner of Sassoferrato and Carlo Dolci, and his picture of St. Peter and St. Paul, while

The Apostles in Art

it has a certain massive dignity, is as devoid of spiritual insight as were the times in which these artists lived. We must associate each phase of art with the moral and social influences that affected it for good or for ill. Guido Reni's St. Peter is a splendid specimen of robust old age, possibly belonging to the powerful merchant class of Italy (p. 82). Paul is perhaps a professor arguing some point in connection with the schools, and is equally remote from the real man. Yet with the pleasant and usually harmonious scheme of colour to which Guido leaned, this is an impressive picture; it is in its representation of saintliness that we perceive failure. It belongs to a period that raised conventionality to an ideal and saw the long, slow ebb of the inspiration that had risen to its height in the Renaissance.

Alonso Cano's full length figure is gentle and dignified but not of great interest. It is typical of a school which with all its genius rarely produced work of religious insight, and was often disfigured by the morbidness that tinged most of the Spanish mystics (p. 73). We are left with the modern example by Mr. Shields. In his graceful panel he has suggested one thought of great significance. St. Paul in his clash with Greek influence, had not only to face the old splendid philosophies and the new smaller ones, but the spirit that was merely whimsical, pleasure-loving, cruel and unclean. The triumph of his teaching meant the overthrow of Pan, that strange fantastic god who, while he was the haunter of wood and stream, was always sinister. Mr. Shields shows him to us at the apostle's feet, prostrate and leering.

Other pictures in which no great attempt has been made to give us a very individual St. Paul, are interesting from the point of view of the representation of an incident. A number are historical, but many were inspired by the numerous traditions the church had cherished and passed on to her children ; indeed, taking the whole dealing of art with the Pauline story it is curious to observe that tradition is chosen more frequently than history, showing its strong hold on the popular mind. The pictures we have under consideration fall naturally into these two classes.

The first to strike us amongst those based on

The Pauline Period

historical sources are the well-known cartoons designed by Raphael for tapestries for the Sistine Chapel. Out of the eleven cartoons of which this series originally consisted only seven remain, and are now in the South Kensington Museum. They are among the most powerful works of this great master. Of the four given in this section perhaps the finest is the St. Paul and Barnabas at Lystra. The two children are beautiful and are typical of the painter, and the architectural background is full of grace. The St. Paul in prison, taken from the tapestry itself (the cartoon has disappeared) is quaint rather than beautiful.

In the French classical school we find some work of importance. The " St. Paul at Ephesus," by Eustache Le Sueur (p. 84), is a dignified picture, finely grouped, which for many years was shown in Notre Dame with some pomp and ceremony on every first of May. The two line-engravings after Poussin are interesting though not very attractive, and his ecstatic vision of St. Paul in which he is caught up to the third heaven, while by no means spiritual in conception, is probably as fine a picture as any that painter produced. The head of the lower angel has real charm (p. 85). A modern French picture of St. Paul at Athens, by Alexandre Bida, while it gives us a quite curiously ineffective St. Paul, has some finely conceived and executed heads among the listening Greeks, particularly the two to the extreme right and left (p. 68). And the listening figures have a distinction that suggests very well a high type of civilization.

It is strange when we consider the romance and adventurousness of St. Paul's missionary career, that some of the hardships, which he catalogues with moving simplicity in the second Epistle to the Corinthians, have not won more artists to depict him. Elsheimer's " St. Paul shipwrecked in Melita," is a picturesque example of the few attempts which have been made, and is characteristic of a period when landscape was beginning to emerge from merely background purposes. There are delicate gradations of distance in it, and the centre is occupied by a graceful hill city of the mediæval type. In strict accordance with the story, the shore is crowded with groups of shipwrecked

The Apostles in Art

folk, and a touch of reality is added by the contrast between the islanders comfortably attired and the rescued passengers, some of them only half clothed, pressing close to the smoking fire (p. 90).

Turning to the pictures which owe their origin to traditional sources, we find of course, a predominance in the martyrdoms. The crowning glory of the saint has always been the call to suffer for the sake of his Lord, and the Church could not rest content without formulating some account of the death of her earliest teachers. Every breath of tradition upon this subject was ardently treasured, and Rome has many churches built upon spots held sacred to such suffering.

By far the finest picture of the martyrdom of St. Paul, is a Tintoretto, and is to be found in that amazing treasure-house the Church of the Madonna dell 'Orto in Venice. It is a picture full of the rapid movement and glory of light which the painter loved. St. Paul, a strong, noble figure, upon whom pain and weariness have left no trace, kneels with his back to us, tense with expectation not of death but of life. His eyes are raised to the swift downrush of the angel who is already bearing to him out of a great radiance the crown and palm of the martyred saint. The Venetian youth to the left, intent upon the blow he is in the act of delivering, is unconscious of the vision and untouched by the light. It is a picture full of the magnificent poetic insight Tintoretto shows in all his work (p. 94).

We cannot help regretting that one painter when at his best did not attempt the representation of St. Paul. Michelangelo, among all the artists of the centuries, was most akin to the great preacher of Christ's Evangel. They were alike in faith, in contempt of earthly comfort, in the strain of poetry which in the artist took the form of perfectly chiselled sonnets, and in the apostle of unpolished but most moving hymns in praise of God and of love. Above all, they were alike in their vehemence and force, that *terribilità*, which perhaps sums up more exactly than any other the natural character of the apostle, the raw material which was transfigured by the grace of Christ into the vast and invincible energy of love which enthroned the Crucified and embraced the world.

St. Paul

ST. PAUL THE APOSTLE. AFTER THE PAINTING AT DRESDEN, FROM A PHOTOGRAPH
BY BRAUN, CLÉMENT & CO., PARIS

Alonso Cano, Spanish School
1601-1667

ST. PAUL

THE APOSTLE PAUL. AFTER THE ORIGINAL PICTURE IN VIENNA, FROM A PHOTOGRAPH BY F. HANFSTAENGL LONDON

Rembrandt, Dutch School
1606-1669

St. Paul

ST. PAUL THE AGED WORN WITH LABOURS, STRIPES, IMPRISON-
MENTS. HE STANDS AS THE AMBASSADOR OF CHRIST TO THE
GENTILES TO TURN THEM FROM DARKNESS UNTO LIGHT,
PREACHING CHRIST CRUCIFIED IN THE ATTITUDE OF SELF-
CRUCIFIXION. AT HIS FEET ARE TWO SYMBOLS: THE GOOD
OLIVE TREE, AND THE GOD PAN, FALLEN AND SHATTERED.
FROM THE PAINTING IN THE CHAPEL OF THE ASCENSION,
BAYSWATER ROAD, LONDON

Frederic Shields, Modern British School

PAUL AND BARNABAS IN CYPRUS

ELYMAS THE SORCERER STRUCK WITH BLINDNESS. "AND NOW, BEHOLD, THE HAND OF THE LORD IS UPON THEE, AND THOU SHALT BE BLIND, NOT SEEING THE SUN FOR A SEASON. AND IMMEDIATELY THERE FELL ON HIM A MIST AND A DARKNESS; AND HE WENT ABOUT SEEKING SOME TO LEAD HIM BY THE HAND." (ACTS XIII., 11.) AFTER THE ORIGINAL CARTOON AT SOUTH KENSINGTON, FROM A PHOTOGRAPH BY THE AUTOTYPE CO., 74, NEW OXFORD STREET, LONDON

Raffaello Sanzio (Raphael of Urbino), Roman School

PAUL AND BARNABAS IN CYPRUS

ST. PAUL AND ST. BARNABAS BEFORE SERGIUS PAULUS: ELYMAS STRUCK WITH BLINDNESS. "AND NOW, BEHOLD, THE HAND OF THE LORD IS UPON THEE, AND THOU SHALT BE BLIND . . ." (ACTS XIII., 11) FROM AN ENGRAVING IN OUTLINE BY MADAME SOYER

Nicolas Poussin, French School
1594-1665

PAUL AND BARNABAS IN LYCAONIA

ST. PAUL AND ST. BARNABAS AT LYSTRA AFTER THE HEALING OF THE CRIPPLE. "THEN THE PRIEST OF JUPITER, WHICH WAS BEFORE THEIR CITY, BROUGHT OXEN AND GARLANDS UNTO THE GATES, AND WOULD HAVE DONE SACRIFICE WITH THE PEOPLE. WHICH WHEN THE APOSTLES, BARNABAS AND PAUL, HEARD OF, THEY RENT THEIR CLOTHES . . . ." (ACTS XIV, 13-14) AFTER THE ORIGINAL CARTOON AT SOUTH KENSINGTON, FROM A PHOTOGRAPH BY THE AUTOTYPE CO., 74, NEW OXFORD STREET, LONDON

Raffaello Sanzio (Raphael of Urbino), Roman School
1483-1520

PAUL AND SILAS AT PHILIPPI IN MACEDONIA

THE SCOURGING OF PAUL AND SILAS. "AND THE MULTITUDE ROSE UP TOGETHER AGAINST THEM: AND THE MAGISTRATES RENT OFF THEIR CLOTHES, AND COMMANDED TO BEAT THEM. AND WHEN THEY HAD LAID MANY STRIPES UPON THEM, THEY CAST THEM INTO PRISON . . ." (ACTS XVI., 22-23.) FROM AN ENGRAVING IN OUTLINE BY MADAME SOYER

Nicolas Poussin, French School
1594-1665

St. Paul at Philippi

ST. PAUL IN PRISON AT PHILIPPI. (ACTS XVI., 26.) THE EARTH-
QUAKE BY WHICH THE PRISON DOORS WERE OPENED IS
HERE REPRESENTED ALLEGORICALLY, AS A TITAN HEAVING UP
THE GROUND. AFTER A TAPESTRY AT ROME, FROM A PHOTO-
GRAPH BY ANDERSON

Raffaello Sanzio (Raphael of Urbino), Roman School
1483-1520

THE INFANT TIMOTHY UNFOLDING THE SCRIPTURES. REPRODUCED FROM A COPYRIGHT MEZZOTINT BY
S. COUSINS, R.A., BY PERMISSION OF HENRY GRAVES & CO.

James Sant, R.A., Modern British School

PAUL AND SILAS AT PHILIPPI

PAUL AND SILAS IN PRISON AT PHILIPPI
(ACTS XVI., 29)
IN THE PRINT ROOM, THE BRITISH MUSEUM

PAUL AND SILAS IN PRISON AT PHILIPPI
DESIGNS FOR THE CUPOLA OF ST. PAUL'S CATHEDRAL, LONDON,

Sir James Thornhill, British School
1676-1734

ST. PETER AND ST. PAUL AT ANTIOCH

THE DISPUTE AT ANTIOCH BETWEEN ST. PETER AND ST. PAUL. "BUT WHEN PETER WAS COME TO ANTIOCH,
I WITHSTOOD HIM TO THE FACE, BECAUSE HE WAS TO BE BLAMED." (GALATIANS II., 11.) AFTER THE
ORIGINAL PAINTING IN THE BRERA, MILAN, FROM A PHOTOGRAPH BY BROGI

Guido Reni, Bolognese School
1575-1642

St. Paul and the Athenians

ST. PAUL AT ATHENS. "AND WHEN THEY HEARD OF THE RESURRECTION OF THE DEAD, SOME MOCKED AND OTHERS SAID, WE WILL HEAR THEE AGAIN OF THIS MATTER.... HOWBEIT CERTAIN MEN CLAVE UNTO HIM, AND BELIEVED." (ACTS XVII., 32, 34). AFTER THE ORIGINAL CARTOON AT SOUTH KENSINGTON, FROM A PHOTOGRAPH BY THE AUTOTYPE CO., 74, NEW OXFORD STREET, LONDON

Raffaello Sanzio (Raphael of Urbino), Roman School
1483-1520

ST. PAUL AT EPHESUS

ST. PAUL AT EPHESUS: THE BURNING OF THE MAGICAL BOOKS. (ACTS XIX., 19.) AFTER THE ORIGINAL
PAINTING IN THE LOUVRE, PARIS, FROM A PHOTOGRAPH BY LÉVY, PARIS

Eustache Le Sueur, French School
1617-1655

St. Paul

THE ECSTATIC VISION OF ST. PAUL, IN WHICH HE WAS CAUGHT UP TO THE THIRD HEAVEN, AND HEARD UNSPEAKABLE WORDS, WHICH IT IS NOT LAWFUL FOR A MAN TO UTTER. (II. CORINTHIANS XII., 2-4.) AFTER THE ORIGINAL PAINTING IN THE LOUVRE, FROM A PHOTOGRAPH BY BRAUN, CLÉMENT & CO., PARIS

Nicolas Poussin, French School
1594-1665

St. Paul at Miletus

ST. PAUL AT MILETUS WITH THE ELDERS OF THE CHURCH OF EPHESUS. "AND THEY ALL WEPT SORE, AND FELL ON PAUL'S NECK, AND KISSED HIM, SORROWING MOST OF ALL FOR THE WORDS WHICH HE SPAKE, THAT THEY SHOULD SEE HIS FACE NO MORE. AND THEY ACCOMPANIED HIM UNTO THE SHIP" (ACTS XX. 37-38). FROM AN ORIGINAL WOODCUT PUBLISHED IN 1860 BY GEORG WIGAND, LEIPZIG

Julius Schnorr, German School

St. Paul in Syria

PAUL AND THE FAITHFUL AT TYRE. "AND THEY ALL BROUGHT US ON OUR WAY, WITH WIVES AND CHILDREN, TILL WE WERE OUT OF THE CITY: AND WE KNEELED DOWN ON THE SHORE, AND PRAYED (ACTS XXI., 5)

Jenny Wylie, Modern British School

ST. PAUL AT CÆSAREA

ST. PAUL BROUGHT TO TRIAL BEFORE FELIX. (ACTS XXIV.) REPRODUCED AFTER AN ORIGINAL SKETCH

Reginald Hallward, Modern British School

ST. PAUL AT CÆSAREA

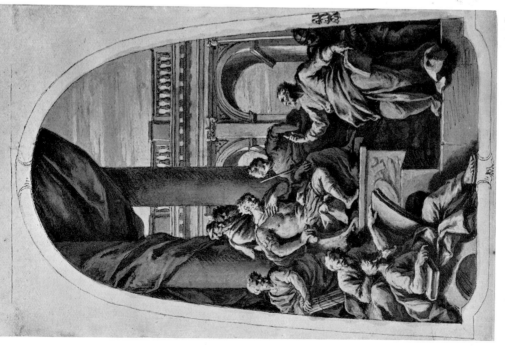

ST. PAUL BEFORE AGRIPPA II. AND HIS SISTER BERENICE. ST. PAUL, BEFORE AGRIPPA II. AND HIS SISTER BERENICE
"THEN AGRIPPA SAID UNTO PAUL, THOU ART PERMITTED TO SPEAK FOR THYSELF. THEN PAUL STRETCHED FORTH THE HAND, AND ANSWERED
FOR HIMSELF. (ACTS XXVI. 1). AFTER THE ORIGINAL DRAWINGS IN THE BRITISH MUSEUM

Sir James Thornhill, British School
1676-1734

St. Paul at Malta

ST. PAUL, SHIPWRECKED ON THE ISLAND CALLED MELITA, IS UNHARMED BY THE VIPER HANGING FROM HIS HAND. "AND WHEN THE BARBARIANS SAW THE VENOMOUS BEAST HANG ON HIS HAND, THEY SAID AMONG THEMSELVES, NO DOUBT THIS MAN IS A MURDERER, WHOM, THOUGH HE HATH ESCAPED THE SEA, YET VENGEANCE SUFFERETH NOT TO LIVE. AND HE SHOOK OFF THE BEAST INTO THE FIRE, AND FELT NO HARM. (ACTS XXVIII, 4-5). AFTER THE ORIGINAL PAINTING IN ST. PETERSBURG, FROM A PHOTOGRAPH BY HANFSTAENGL, LONDON

Adam Elsheimer, German School

St. Paul in Rome

ONESIPHORUS VISITING ST. PAUL IN THE ROMAN PRISON. "THE LORD GIVE MERCY UNTO THE HOUSE OF ONESIPHORUS; FOR HE OFT REFRESHED ME, AND WAS NOT ASHAMED OF MY CHAIN: BUT, WHEN HE WAS IN ROME, HE SOUGHT ME OUT VERY DILIGENTLY, AND FOUND ME." (II. TIMOTHY I., 16-17)

Reginald Hallward, Modern British School

A LEGENDARY INCIDENT IN THE LIVES OF ST. PETER AND ST. PAUL, RECORDED IN THE GOLDEN LEGEND, AND SHOWING THE RAISING OF THE KING'S SON IN THE COURT OF THE PALACE AT ANTIOCH. THE ILLUSTRATION REPRESENTS THE CENTRAL PORTION OF THE SUBJECT, WHERE ST. PETER BIDS THE DEAD CHILD OF THEOPHILUS TO ARISE, WHILE ST. PAUL KNEELS IN PRAYER IN THE MIDST OF THE COURTIERS. . . . AFTER A FRESCO IN THE BRANCACCI CHAPEL, FLORENCE. REPRODUCED FROM A PHOTOGRAPH BY ANDERSON

Begun by Masaccio (1401-1428), Florentine School
Finished by Filippino Lippi, Florentine School
About 1457-1504

ST. PAUL AT ROME. AS WHEN HE DWELT FOR TWO WHOLE YEARS IN HIS OWN HOUSE, CHAINED BY THE WRIST TO HIS SOLDIER GUARD. THE APOSTLE IS PLEADING WITH A CENTURION OF THE PRÆTORIAN GUARD, AND PRESSING THE GRACE OF GOD IN CHRIST SO EARNESTLY THAT THE OFFICER IS DEEPLY MOVED. BEHIND, ST. LUKE KNEELS IN PRAYER. FROM THE ORIGINAL PICTURE IN THE CHAPEL OF ASCENSION, BAYSWATER ROAD, LONDON

Frederic Shields, Modern British School

LEGENDARY

ST. PETER AND ST. PAUL LED TO PRISON IN ROME. AFTER THE ORIGINAL PAINTING IN THE UFFIZI GALLERY,
FLORENCE, FROM A PHOTOGRAPH BY ANDERSON, ROME

Hans von Kulmbach, German School
Died 1522

TRADITIONAL

THE BEHEADING OF ST. PAUL. AFTER THE ORIGINAL PAINTING AT VENICE, IN THE
CHURCH OF THE MADONNA DELL'ORTO FROM A PHOTOGRAPH BY ANDERSON, ROME

Jacopo Robusti (il Tintoretto), Venetian School
1519-1594

TRADITIONAL

THE MARTYRDOM OF ST. PAUL. AFTER THE ORIGINAL DRAWING IN THE LOUVRE, PARIS, FROM A PHOTOGRAPH
BY BRAUN, CLEMENT & CO., PARIS

Giuseppe Cesari, Neapolitan School
1560(?)-1640

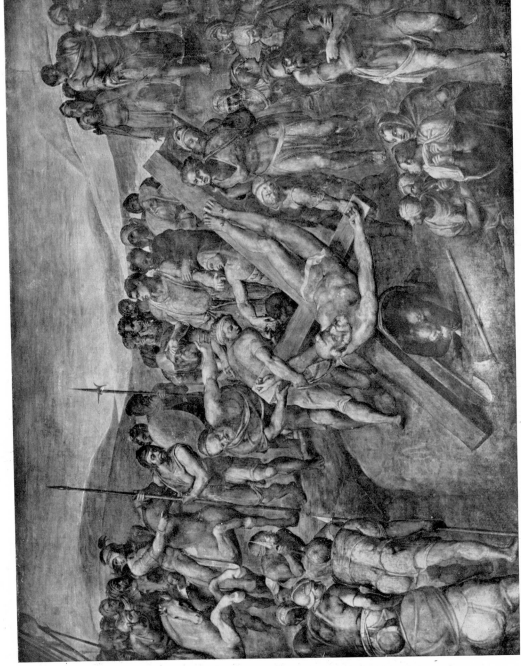

TRADITIONAL

THE CRUCIFIXION OF ST. PETER. AFTER THE ORIGINAL FRESCO IN THE CAPPELLA PAOLINA, ROME. THE PHOTOGRAPH BY ALINARI

Michelangelo Buonarroti, Florentine School
1475-1564

TRADITIONAL

THE MARTYRDOM OF ST. PETER. AFTER THE PICTURE IN THE
BRUSSELS GALLERY. THE PHOTOGRAPH BY W. A. MANSELL

Sir Anthony Van Dyck, Flemish School
1599-1641

THE MARTYRDOM OF ST. PETER. AFTER THE PICTURE AT ROME IN THE
CORSINI GALLERY. THE PHOTOGRAPH BY ANDERSON

Guido Reni, Bolognese School
1575-1642

LEGENDARY

ST. PHILIP EXORCISING THE DRAGON. THIS PICTURE, IN S. Mª NOVELLA, FLORENCE, REPRESENTS A LEGEND WHICH RECORDS HOW ST. PHILIP, WHEN PREACHING AT HIEROPOLIS, IN PHRYGIA, FOUND THAT THE PEOPLE WORSHIPPED THE GOD MARS UNDER THE FORM OF A HUGE DRAGON. THE APOSTLE COMMANDED THE CREATURE TO DISAPPEAR, AND THE DRAGON CAME FROM BEHIND THE ALTAR, EMITTING A SMELL SO POISONOUS THAT THE KING'S SON FELL DEAD IN THE ARMS OF HIS ATTENDANTS. REPRODUCED FROM A PHOTOGRAPH BY ANDERSON, ROME

Filippino Lippi Florentine School

LEGENDARY

THE APOSTLE ST. PHILIP WITH HIS CROSS. ACCORDING TO THE ANCIENT GREEK TRADITIONS ST. PHILIP WAS
CRUCIFIED WITH HIS HEAD DOWNWARDS, LIKE ST. PETER. AFTER THE ORIGINAL PICTURE IN THE LOUVRE,
PARIS, FROM A PHOTOGRAPH BY BRAUN, CLEMENT & CO.

Philippe de Champaigne, Flemish School
1602-1674

LEGENDARY

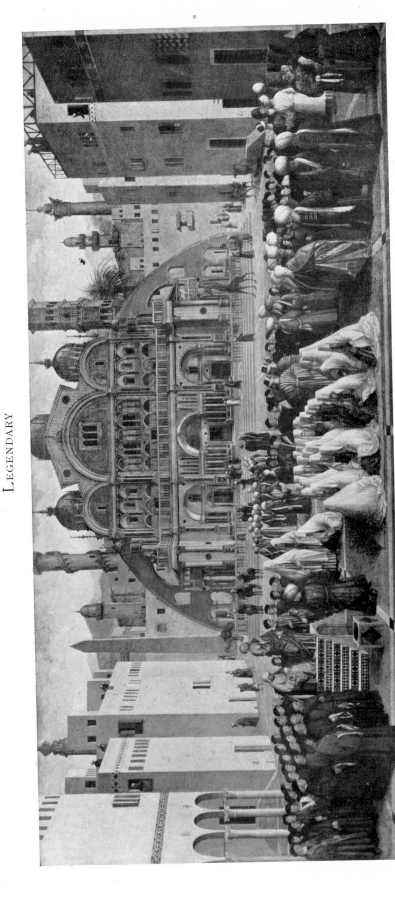

ST. MARK PREACHING THE GOSPEL AT ALEXANDRIA. AFTER THE ORIGINAL PICTURE IN THE BRERA AT MILAN, FROM A COPYRIGHT PHOTOGRAPH BY ALINARI, FLORENCE

Gentile Bellini, Venetian School
About 1426-7-1507

ST. JUDE PROCLAIMING THE AWFUL JUDGMENT OF GOD
RESERVED FOR PROFLIGATE TEACHERS AND FALSE
PASTORS. FROM THE ORIGINAL PAINTING IN THE
CHAPEL OF THE ASCENSION, BAYSWATER ROAD, LONDON

Frederic Shields, Modern British School

LEGENDARY

THE MARTYRDOM OF ST. MARK. THE LEGEND SAYS THAT ST. MARK, DURING THE FEAST OF THE GOD SERAPIS, WAS DRAGGED THROUGH THE STREETS OF ALEXANDRIA BY THE ANGRY POPULACE, WHO PULLED HIM ALONG BY A ROPE, TILL AT LAST A GREAT STORM OF HAIL FELL UPON HIS MURDERERS AND DESTROYED THEM. FROM THE PICTURE IN THE UFFIZI GALLERY, THE PHOTOGRAPH BY ANDERSON, ROME

Fra Angelico da Fiesole, Florentine School
1387-1455

A COMPOSITE PICTURE REPRESENTING TWO TRADITIONAL INCIDENTS. ON THE LEFT, THE MARTYRDOM OF ST. PETER. ON THE RIGHT, ST. PETER AND ST. PAUL ARE ACCUSED BEFORE NERO BY SIMON MAGUS. AFTER THE FRESCO IN THE CARMINE, FLORENCE, THE PHOTOGRAPH BY ANDERSON, ROME

Filippino Lippi, Florentine School
1457-1504

LEGENDARY

THE TRADITIONAL MARTYRDOM OF ST. ANDREW ON HIS TRANSVERSE CROSS. ACCORDING TO THE LEGEND
ST. ANDREW CAME BY HIS DEATH AT PATRAS BECAUSE HE HAD PERSUADED MAXIMILLA, WIFE OF THE PROCONSUL
ÆGEUS, TO MAKE A PUBLIC CONFESSION OF CHRISTIANITY. THE LEGEND ALSO RELATES HOW ST. ANDREW,
BEFORE HIS MARTYRDOM, ADORED THE CROSS, KNEELING HUMBLY, IN MEMORY OF THE REDEEMER'S SACRIFICE. THE
ILLUSTRATION REPRESENTS A PICTURE IN THE PITTI GALLERY, FLORENCE, AFTER A PHOTOGRAPH BY BRAUN,
CLÉMENT & CO., PARIS

Carlo Dolci, Florentine School
1616-1686

In the Times of Nero

THE CATACOMBS AND THE EARLIEST TIMES OF THE CHRISTIAN CHURCH IN ROME. AFTER THE ORIGINAL
CARTOON IN THE MUSÉE DE LYON, FROM A PHOTOGRAPH BY BRAUN, CLÉMENT & CO., PARIS

Paul Chenavard, Modern French School
Died 1895

In the Times of Nero

CHRISTIAN MARTYRS. AFTER THE ORIGINAL PAINTING AT NAPLES, IN THE CAPODIMONTE MUSEUM, FROM A PHOTOGRAPH BY E. BROGI

Domenico Morelli, Modern Italian School

St. John and the Apocalypse

By the Rev. R. J. Campbell, M.A.

WHEN we think of St. John the Divine, the Apostle of Love, we feel that he has impressed the Christian imagination more potently, perhaps, than any other member of the apostolic band. He is remembered as the disciple whom Jesus loved, and tradition dwells upon his winsomeness of character and his insistence upon the primary duty of loving our fellowmen if we would know God. Above all, the mysticism and wonderful spiritual insight of the Gospel attributed to him have helped to endear St. John to all followers of his Master, especially to those whose religious experience is of the quality which the fourth Gospel stimulates and satisfies. But none of these influences, or all combined, can quite account for the affectionate reverence paid by Christians to the memory of St. John. Nothing in the fourth Gospel, the Johannine Epistles, or the Apocalypse, surpasses in tender spiritual beauty the teaching about love contained I Cor., xiii; and yet, somehow, we do not think of the massive personality of the Apostle Paul in quite the same terms as we do of St. John. The truth is we know the latter more from tradition than from the printed page, while the former owes his influence chiefly to the intellectual and spiritual force of his recorded ideas. Protestants, perhaps, do not allow enough for tradition. Tradition has often more to do with the making of our impressions than has the written word. It works by means of subtle psychological forces, transmitting impressions from one generation to another, and dealing mainly with facts to which ordinary language is unequal. This is how we have come to know St. John. He possessed the precious gift of personality, that mysterious, but unescapable force which plays so great a part in the affairs of men; and tradition has preserved for us something of its power. The scent

The Apostles in Art

of violets will linger around a casket which once contained the actual flowers for years after the flowers themselves are gone. So it is with the memory of a great man. What he actually was somehow passes into the general consciousness of the race or the spiritual society to which he belongs ; and thus, despite the paucity of historical evidence, the Christian world will go on believing that it knows St. John, the man himself, the intimate friend and companion of Jesus; and the probabilities are that the Christian world is right.

And yet how little we know of the veritable life history of this apostle. The synoptic writers refer to him as one of three who were amongst the earliest to become the followers of Jesus. Luke tells with some fulness of detail the story of the call of the brothers James and John to become fishers of men ; Matthew and Mark briefly record the same fact. Probably the call was not so abrupt as the terse gospel narrative makes it appear. The brothers may often have heard Jesus speak ; it is even possible that they may have already possessed an intimate lifelong acquaintance with him, because tradition speaks of their mother Salome as the sister of our Lord. At any rate their active interest in the new teacher and the good news of the kingdom must have preceded his invitation to them to prepare for new and higher work. Their father, Zebedee, appears to have been fairly well to do ; he possessed hired servants, some of whom were present at the time when the brothers left the ships to follow Jesus. Zebedee may have been the owner of a small fleet of shipping boats on the Galilean lake. It is often taken for granted that our Lord must have belonged to the poorer classes, but the assumption is scarcely justifiable from the hints which are given in the New Testament as to His circumstances and connections. Lazarus, for example, evidently belonged to the circle which supplied the social and ecclesiastical leaders of Jerusalem, a circle which, though in the end hostile to Jesus, was at one time disposed to regard Him with favour. The mother of the sons of Zebedee was one of the group of women who ministered to Jesus during His journeys, no doubt with the approval, and from the bounty,

St. John and the Apocalypse

of the husband and father. So far as one can judge, the class to which all these people belonged, though not of outstanding importance, was not poor ; and Professor Ramsay has pointed out, in his suggestive little book on the Education of Christ, that the Galilean youth at this time was one of the best educated in the world. What we can see, therefore, of the childhood and early manhood of St. John points to the fact that his circumstances were such as to afford him a certain preparation for the great work to which he was afterwards called. His forbears were simple God-fearing people, able and willing to have him instructed in the scriptures and history of ancient Israel. Like so many of their class they shared in the dream of a restored kingdom wherein righteousness and joy should dwell. The indirect testimony of the gospels is to the effect that the whole household of Zebedee might be accounted among the adherents of Jesus, the prophet of the better day that was dawning.

James and John, during the great three years' ministry, were the constant companions of Jesus in association with a third person who has become known to history as the Apostle Peter, and whose influence from the point of view of ecclesiastical theory has been much greater than that of St. John. If, as seems probable enough from the several references in the Gospels, it was our Lord's wish that Peter should assume a certain official primacy over the newly founded society, it seems equally certain that John was admitted to a certain specially sacred fellowship with Himself. Not once is John mentioned by name in the fourth gospel, a fact which is not without a certain significance, because the purposeful silence of the writer regarding John is evidence enough of intention to give him the principal credit for the authorship of the book. Perhaps we need say no more than this. Whoever wrote the book it is clear that he means to designate St. John by the beautiful phrase, " The disciple whom Jesus loved." The book is first and foremost a spiritual treatise, not a history. It assumes a knowledge of Matthew, Mark and Luke, but draws also upon another source for an intimate knowledge of the words and the acts of Jesus

The Apostles in Art

at certain solemn crises, particularly during the last stages of His life on earth. What else can this be but John's memoirs, oral or literary (probably the former), of his beloved Lord? In this marvellously able book the primacy of Peter is well brought out, especially in the last chapter, but no less so is the sweet intimacy which must have existed between Jesus and John. Perhaps the phrase, "the disciple whom Jesus loved," means no more in the mouth of the evangelist than the self-designation, "Christ's poor little one, Francis," meant in the mouth of the founder of the Franciscan order. In either case it was an expression of gratitude, not a claim to superior merit or special favour. The whole tone of the gospel is inconsistent with the supposition that the writer desires to draw special attention to the personality of St. John. The literary device of omitting his name is obvious enough, but throughout the whole history no attempt is made to claim for him any position of prominence in the conduct of affairs.

But was this always so? Hardly. On comparing the three Synoptic Gospels with the fourth we are able to trace a remarkable amount of character development in the history of John, and had it not been for this development his influence upon Christendom might have been vastly different from what it is. The three outstanding figures of the apostolic band, Peter, James and John, are frequently stated to have been called upon to accompany Jesus on occasions when others were excluded. Such were the raising of Jairus' daughter, the Transfiguration on the Mount, and the agony in Gethsemane. The three, therefore, were evidently regarded as being more fully in the counsels of the Master than were the remainder of His not inconsiderable following. A certain amount of rivalry, therefore, arose between the brothers and Peter, the cause of which is not far to seek. One of the greatest difficulties of the Master was that of removing from the minds of His followers certain mistaken prepossessions regarding the meaning of the kingdom of God and His own relation to it. The mind of the Jewish people at this time was greatly occupied with fervent anticipations concerning the near advent

THE FOUR HORSES OF THE APOCALYPSE AND THEIR RIDERS. AFTER THE ORIGINAL CARTOON, DESIGNED FOR A PROJECTED
CAMPO SANTO AT BERLIN, REPRODUCED BY PERMISSION OF THE BERLIN PHOTOGRAPHIC CO., LONDON

Peter von Cornelius, German School
1783-1867

St. John and the Apocalypse

of this divine kingdom. Their religious leaders, and the official interpreters of their scriptures, kept the idea constantly before them and encouraged fervent anticipations of the greatness and gladness of Israel in the good time coming. The causes of this popular expectation lay chiefly in the political conditions of the moment and the wide diffusion of Messianic literature. Palestine was now a part of the Roman Empire, and broken up into several minor governments, each paying its tribute to Cæsar. There were hardships and many humiliations to endure, although Rome was tolerant of national manners and customs, and even of religion, except when it encouraged political unrest. Subject races, within certain limitations, were permitted even to retain their own laws. But Israel looked wistfully back to a period of national splendour and prosperity, longing for a restoration of the military glory of David, and all that the name of that great prince suggested. The nation had never recovered from the Babylonian captivity in the 6th century B.C. Since that event, indeed, it had passed through a succession of tribulations ; now it was comprehended in the world-embracing empire of Rome. We cannot marvel, therefore, that men of patriotic spirit should have dreamed of a great national deliverance to be wrought out by a heaven-sent leader. They looked for the overthrow of Rome, and for a corresponding exaltation of the Jewish race to something like universal dominion. This change was to come suddenly and completely, and the effect was to be the establishment of a kingdom of righteousness, peace, and plenty. To most of the contemporaries of Jesus this was what was meant by the kingdom of God, but to Him the idea meant something more. No doubt He believed in the possibility of realizing an ideal condition of things on earth, but He believed the change would come within men themselves before it came without. A kingdom inaugurated by violence and maintained by force was not to his mind. His view was that the kingdom had come already in the heart of any man who sought to do the will of God and who was filled with love for mankind. But the difficulty was to make his contemporaries understand this. The

The Apostles in Art

contrast between their notion of the kingdom and his was immense. They thought of a cataclysm, Jesus of a process; they of a violent overthrow of the enemies of Israel, He of a change in the inner man; they thought of a kingdom wholly of this world, He of a kingdom embracing both heaven and earth; they expected a mighty conqueror as their national Messiah, He represented almost the very opposite ideal.

It might be supposed that, despite the difficulty of eradicating false ideas from the popular mind, our Lord would succeed better with his immediate followers. To a certain extent, of course, he did, but the work was slow. So possessed were these simple Galileans by the idea that their Master would presently establish an earthly kingdom that they seem to have begun to distribute the offices beforehand. And here we get a glimpse of an element in the character of John which is not to be found in the later John of Christian tradition, *viz.*, worldly ambition. He and his brother James sought to forestall Peter and to secure from their Master the promise that in the coming kingdom they should be permitted to occupy the places of principal dignity next to his own. In one account it is their mother who is represented as requesting the favour on their behalf, but in any case the rest of the apostolic band disapproved of the attempt and were angry with the brothers. The bickering thus occasioned seems actually to have continued until the eve of the arrest of Jesus; more than once there was strife among them as to who should be the greatest, and at the last supper itself the Master found it necessary by means of the acted parable of the foot-washing to impress upon the minds of his followers that love was the great ideal. This, as we should expect, is best brought out in the fourth Gospel, which probably embodies John's account of the matter and shows us something of the great change which must have taken place in the disposition of the man, for ambition is the last thing to be associated with him in the years that followed the tragedy of Calvary. It is noteworthy that in the closing chapters of the fourth Gospel, as well as in the Petrine sections in the Acts of the Apostles, Peter and John are shown in close

St. John and the Apocalypse

association. Apparently John possessed some acquaintance with the family of the high priest, for it is through his mediation that Peter gains admission to the hall of Caiaphas ; he and Peter come together to the empty tomb ; later on they go fishing together on lake Tiberias, and John is present—for no doubt John is meant—when Peter receives his final commission to tend the sheep and feed the lambs of the flock of Christ. A beautiful touch is introduced here, well worth a representation in sacred art. Instead of grasping at precedence, as he would have done in earlier days, John is represented as following behind Peter at the close of this recorded conversation, while Peter on his part seems anxious that his comrade should take the lead. Jesus gives to both their place ; the one is to be the leader and spokesman of the little community, the other is to have a longer if less conspicuous ministry. In the " Acts " Peter and John are shown working and suffering together. The story of the miracle at the beautiful gate of the Temple, and the events which followed immediately thereon, exhibit both apostles in a pleasing light. They have been praying together ; Peter pronounces the healing word over the paralytic and defends the work when he and his friend are arrested ; but both are imprisoned and maltreated, the silent John taking his full share of the consequences of Peter's action.

There are other hints in the New Testament of a difference between the earlier and the later John. At one time, incensed at the contemptuous treatment of their Master, the sons of Zebedee wished to call down fire from heaven to consume the offenders. Perhaps the name Boanerges, by which they were known to the apostolic band, may have been suggested by this and similar incidents. The designation " Sons of Thunder " would not be inappropriate at this time. On another occasion they peremptorily interfered to prohibit a man from performing works of healing in their Master's name. There is just one traditional instance of the persistence of something of this characteristic in the St. John of after years, namely, his vehement repudiation of Cerinthus the arch-heretic. Eusebius, that careful ecclesiastical historian, tells the story thus :

The Apostles in Art

" It is highly probable that Cerinthus, the same that established the heresy that bears his name, designedly affixed the name (of John) to his own forgery. For one of the doctrines that he taught was, that Christ would have an earthly kingdom. And as he was a voluptuary, and altogether sensual, he conjectured that it would consist in those things that he craved in the gratification of appetite and lust ; *i.e.*, in eating, drinking, and marrying, or in such things whereby he supposed these sensual pleasures might be presented in more decent expressions, *viz.*, in festivals, sacrifices and the slaying of victims. Irenaeus, in his first book against heresies, adds certain false doctrines of the man, though kept more secret, and gives a history in his third book, that deserves to be recorded, as received by tradition from Polycarp. He says that John the apostle once entered a bath to wash ; but ascertaining Cerinthus was within, he leaped out of the place, and fled from the door, not enduring to enter under the same roof with him, and exhorted those with him to do the same, saying, ' Let us flee, lest the bath fall in, as long as Cerinthus, that enemy of truth, is within.' "

If this presentation of the teaching of Cerinthus be approximately correct, the horror of the apostle was not without some justification. But the glimpse it gives of St. John's character coincides with what we can gather from the New Testament narratives. Evidently his was an intense, loving, passionate nature with the defects of its qualities. His ardent loyalty to a name or a truth would occasionally carry him into intolerance. The effect of the personality of Jesus upon such a disposition must have been elevating and ennobling ; without that influence such a disposition might have run into the extremes of egoism and worldliness. But from the first Jesus must have seen the latent possibilities in the character of His follower. The rebuke He administered to the youth's ambition took the form of a question, Are ye able to drink of the cup that I am about to drink ? To John's eager affirmative He further responded, My cup indeed ye shall drink. Jesus knew his disciple better than John knew himself.

If tradition be trustworthy John was the youngest of the apostolic band and specially attached to his master's person. He appears to have been the only one of the eleven present at the Crucifixion and to his care was committed the mother of Jesus. This alone shows us something of the intimate

St. John and the Apocalypse

personal relationship which must have existed between Jesus and John. Whether the words of the fourth Gospel are in this instance to be accepted literally or not, the fact remains that John was the one of the apostolic band to whom such a commission could most fitly be entrusted. A curious turn of phrase at the close of the fourth Gospel is probably intended as a contemporary attestation of the trustworthiness of the recorded incidents following upon the passion of Jesus :—" This is the disciple which testifieth of these things, and wrote these things : and *we* know that his testimony is true." Evidently John is not the writer of the account in its present form ; he is the authority behind it. Who the " we " are does not appear. Is there not here a suggestion of the fact about which later tradition is so persistent, namely, that the apostle at Ephesus gathered about him a school of able followers ? May it not have been that the fourth Gospel issued from this school ? The note of intimacy in the book, particularly in the chapters on the last hours of Jesus before the betrayal, is thus accounted for without supposing John to have been the actual writer of the whole.

There is little further reference to the personality of St. John in the New Testament. St. Paul, in the Epistle to the Galatians, mentions him as being present at the council of Jerusalem and as being a pillar of the church. But sub-apostolic tradition has a great deal to say concerning his later life. Unfortunately the lines of the tradition are not entirely consistent, and there is even some question as to a possible confusion of identity with another John who seems to have been described as John the Elder. But in the main the churches held that, after the termination of St. Paul's mission in Asia Minor, the Apostle John settled in Ephesus and exercised a kind of patriarchal jurisdiction over the churches of the whole province. Our principal authority for this statement is Irenaeus, who refers to the fact frequently in his writings. He tells us indeed that in his own early childhood he was a pupil of Polycarp and had often heard his teacher speaking of the Apostle John. Polycarp must have been a very old man at the time Irenaeus listened to him, and a

The Apostles in Art

very young one when he knew the apostle, but his witness is valuable and has the appearance of being genuine. We have here a link between actual history and apostolic times. Some historical critics hold that the John whom Polycarp knew was not the apostle, but the elder. As to this, however, tradition, though not absolutely clear, throws the greater weight of testimony on the side of Irenaeus. Polycrates, in 196 A.D., writing to Victor, Bishop of Rome, states that the John who lay on the bosom of the Lord was buried in Ephesus. The often-quoted testimony of Papias is not so conclusive, for he speaks of both Johns with reverence and regard. On the whole there is a strong presumption in favour of the view that the apostle actually did spend the closing years of his life in Ephesus and exercised considerable influence from that centre. It seems unquestionable, too, that the literary output of the Ephesian Christians was considerable. Of the works attributed to St. John, or composed under his influence, the fourth Gospel and the Apocalypse are the chief, together with the three letters which stand in his name. But no doubt a voluminous literature from this prolific school has been lost. The Apocalypse, indeed, supplies an indirect testimony in favour of St. John's presence at Ephesus, for the letters to the several churches at the commencement of the work are plainly written by one who is entitled to assume considerable moral authority over those he addresses. Whether the rest of the book is apostolic, and whether it is a unity at all is a much disputed question. It was widely recognised in the church of the 2nd century, but in the 3rd the Johannine authorship began to be questioned. Eusebius, for example, attributes the book to John the Elder. After the Reformation the question was raised again, when Luther and others cast doubt upon the authorship. Whoever the author may have been the book is a striking production of the Johannine school. No book in the New Testament canon has been more fantastically interpreted. Protestant exegesis, for instance, has commonly identified the Scarlet Woman with the church of Rome, and explanations equally baseless have been given of many of the other symbols employed

St. John and the Apocalypse

in the work. It may as well be admitted that many of the allusions it contains are lost upon modern readers, for the simple reason that west and too far from the events indicated and that our mental dialect is so vastly different. If, a thousand years hence, some member of the English-speaking race were to come upon a copy of to-day's *Times* he might be impressed by the style of the leading articles, but many of the allusions made and the symbols employed would be obscure to him because of the changes wrought in the intervening millennium. We have to allow for a similar fact in our study of the Apocalypse. It belongs to an era and a race whose literary thought-forms were quite different from our own. The writer is addressing Christians of Jewish race, and assumes them to be familiar with the figures he employs, as doubtless they were. It belongs to the same order as the book of Daniel, and perhaps was modelled upon it. How many apocalypses were in circulation at the time we have no means of knowing, but doubtless there was a considerable number. The symbols employed in such literature were intended to serve much the same purpose as the illustrations in modern magazines ; they focussed the reader's attention and brought out the most important parts of the author's meaning.

Looked at from this point of view, the Apocalypse becomes a very human document. It is intensely dramatic and passionate. Evidently it was written at a time when the Christians were undergoing fierce persecution ; probably, therefore, it appeared in the reign of Nero or Domitian. It should be remembered that to the author the Roman Empire is synonymous with civilisation ; to him it is the world, and to him the spirit of imperial Rome is the spirit against which Christianity has to contend. It was a cruel old world, luxury-loving, vicious, sensual, depraved, materialized, superstitious. The Christians were required to show their loyalty to the established order by rendering divine honours to the reigning Cæsar. Their refusal to do this was punished as treason. The point of view of the author of the Apocalypse is therefore quite clear. He sees that a deadly conflict is being waged between the old order and the new, and that the

The Apostles in Art

pagan civilisation of Rome must in the end give way before the cross. This is the real Armageddon of history. By the beast with the mystic number 666 he means Cæsar, and by the Scarlet Woman he means the imperial City herself, drunk with the blood of the saints. His indebtedness to the book of Daniel as a literary model is evident from his use of the word Babylon to describe the city which was now the centre of the world. There was, therefore, nothing so very wonderful about the nature of the prophecy, which in all essentials has been fulfilled. Not a few thoughtful, intelligent men were then reading the signs of the times in a similar way. The Apocalypse is not more severe than Tacitus, for instance, in its condemnation of the manners of the empire. The forces which were ere long to work the over- throw of the mighty world-wide dominion were already operating, and in a few generations they produced their fell effect. What the writer of the Apocalypse predicted then came to pass. Out of the chaos a new civilisation was born and was cradled by the Christian Church. Our modern civilisation owes more to Christianity than to any moral force whatsoever. It has sinister elements and dark and fearful problems, but we may thank God that men are not as men were in the days of Cæsar. It was this great change which the writer of the Apocalypse foresaw, with the vision of a mystic and a statesman. That his thoughts are clothed in a form to which we are not now accustomed detracts nothing from the interest of the work. It tells of a turning point in the world's history, a great and solemn moment fraught with weal or woe for the ages yet to come. The seer knew this and set such a high value upon his words that he peremptorily forbade any modification of them. It would be worth something if we could know what was their effect upon the churches during the time of suffering to which they refer. Concerning this period the ecclesiastical historian tells us :—

> "In this persecution, it is handed down by tradition, that the apostle and evangelist John, who was yet living, in consequence of his testimony to the divine word, was condemned to dwell on the island of Patmos. Irenaeus, indeed, in his fifth book against the heresies, where he speaks of the calculation formed on the epithet of Anti-Christ,

THE APOCALYPSE

(REVELATION vi., 12.)

IN THE NATIONAL GALLERY OF IRELAND

THE OPENING OF THE SIXTH SEAL

Francis Danby, A.R.A., British School
1793 (?)—1861

St. John and the Apocalypse

in the above-mentioned Revelation of John, speaks in the following manner respecting him. ' If, however, it were necessary to proclaim (*i.e.*, Anti-Christ) openly at the present time, it would have been declared by him who saw the revelation, for it is not long since it was seen, but almost in our own generation, at the close of Domitian's reign.' To such a degree, indeed, did the doctrine which we profess flourish, that even historians who are very far from befriending our religion have not hesitated to record this persecution and its martyrdoms in their histories. These, also, have accurately noted the time, for it happened, according to them, in the fifteenth year of Domitian."

Dionysius of Alexandria, a distinguished prelate and a high authority in that great intellectual centre in the 3rd century, refers the Apocalypse to another John than the son of Zebedee. Whether this view is the correct one or not it is surely safe to assume that Ephesus was the chief centre of the Johannine school, and that the traditional association of John the Apostle with that centre is not without some measure of probability.

A considerable amount of legend gathers round the later career of the apostle. There is, indeed, in the chronicle of Georgios Hamartolos a statement to the effect that John suffered martyrdom after writing his gospel ; the chronicle makes this statement on the alleged authority of Papias and Origen, but nothing is said about it elsewhere. The main current of tradition goes to show that the apostle lived to an advanced age. He was perhaps saved by being exiled to Patmos during the persecution with which the Apocalypse is concerned. Attempts are said to have been made to put him to death, one by means of a cup of poison, and another by immersing him in a cauldron of boiling oil, but he miraculously escaped unhurt. He is supposed to have worked many notable miracles, the accounts of some of of which are rather childish. For example, it is stated that on one occasion he found his bed infested with vermin in a certain inn where he was staying for the night. Forthwith he ordered them out, after the manner of St. Patrick with the poisonous serpents. In the morning the excluded visitors were all found waiting on the doorstep until the saint should allow them to return ! We have it on the authority of Tertullian that he

The Apostles in Art

visited Rome, whence he barely escaped with his life. At Ephesus he is said to have raised a woman from the dead. Cassian tells us that in extreme old age he amused himself frequently by playing with a tame partridge. One day a huntsman passing by with his bow and arrows expressed astonishment at seeing the great apostle, so venerable for age and sanctity, thus amusing himself. The apostle asked him if he kept his bow always bent. The huntsman answered, " That would be the way to render it useless." " If," replied St. John, "you unbend your bow to prevent it being useless, I unbend my mind for the same reason." Another story is that two young men, who had sold all their possessions to follow him, afterwards repented. He sent them to gather pebbles and faggots, and on their return changed these into nuggets of gold, saying " Take back your riches, as you regret having exchanged them for heaven." A further story has it that when the time of his departure drew near he caused a grave to be dug and lay down in it. On the morrow his body was found to have disappeared, having ascended like his master's to heaven. Another tradition declared that he was not dead, but only asleep waiting until the consummation of all things, which was supposed to be near at hand, when he would awake to share in the triumph of his Lord without being called upon to pass through the experience of death at all.

Perhaps the two most beautiful legends concerning him are those of the recovery of the robber chief and of his habitual benediction to the church. The former is told by Clement, of Alexandria, as follows :

" Listen to a story that is no fiction, but a real history, handed down and carefully preserved, respecting the Apostle John. For after the tyrant was dead, coming from the isle of Patmos to Ephesus, he went also, when called, to the neighbouring regions of the Gentiles ; in some to appoint bishops, in some to institute entire new churches, in others to appoint to the ministry some one of those that were pointed out by the Holy Ghost. When he came, therefore, to one of those cities, at no great distance, of which some also give the name, and had in other respects consoled his brethren, he at last turned towards the bishop ordained (appointed), and seeing a youth of fine stature, graceful

St. John and the Apocalypse

countenance, and ardent mind, he said, ' Him I commend to you with all earnestness, in the presence of the church and of Christ.' The bishop having taken him and promised all, he repeated and testified the same thing, and then returned to Ephesus. The presbyter, taking the youth home that was committed to him, educated, restrained, and cherished him, and at length baptized him. After this, he relaxed exercising his former care and vigilance, as if he had now committed him to a perfect safeguard in the seal of the Lord. But certain idle, dissolute fellows, familiar with every kind of wickedness, unhappily attach themselves to him, thus prematurely freed from restraint. At first they lead him on by expensive entertainments. Then going out at night to plunder, they take him with them. Next, they encourage him to something greater, and gradually becoming accustomed to their ways, in his enterprising spirit, like an unbridled and powerful steed that has struck out of the right way, biting the curb, he rushed with so much the greater impetuosity towards the precipice. At length, renouncing the salvation of God, he contemplated no trifling offence, but having committed some great crime, since he was now once ruined, he expected to suffer equally with the rest. Taking, therefore, these same associates, and forming them into a band of robbers, he became their captain, surpassing them all in violence, blood, and cruelty. Time elapsed, and on a certain occasion they send for John. The Apostle, after appointing those other matters for which he came, said, ' Come, bishop, return me my deposit, which I and Christ committed to thee, in the presence of the church over which thou dost preside.' The bishop at first, indeed, was confounded, thinking that he was insidiously charged for money which he had not received ; and yet he could neither give credit respecting that which he had not, nor yet disbelieve John. But when he said, ' I demand the young man, and the soul of a brother,' the old man, groaning heavily and also weeping, said, ' He is dead.' ' How, and what death ? ' ' He is dead to God,' said he. ' He has turned out wicked and abandoned, and at last a robber ; and now, instead of the church, he has beset the mountain with a band like himself.' The Apostle, on hearing this, tore his garment, and beating his head with great lamentation, said, ' I left a fine keeper of a brother's soul ! But let a horse now be got ready, and some one to guide me on my way.' He rode as he was, away from the church, and coming to the country, was taken prisoner by the outguard of the banditti. He neither attempted, however, to flee, nor refused to be taken ; but cried out, ' For this very purpose am I come ; conduct me to your captain.' He, in the mean time, stood waiting, armed as he was. But as he recognised John advancing towards him,

The Apostles in Art

overcome with shame he turned about to flee. The Apostle, however, pursued him with all his might, forgetful of his age, and crying out, ' Why dost thou fly, my son, from me, thy father ; thy defenceless, aged father ? Have compassion on me, my son ; fear not. Thou still hast hope of life. I will intercede with Christ for thee. Should it be necessary, I will cheerfully suffer death for thee, as Christ did. I will give my life for thine. Stay ; believe Christ hath sent me.' Hearing this, he at first stopped with downcast looks. Then threw away his arms ; then trembling, lamented bitterly, and embracing the old man as he came up attempted to plead for himself with his lamentations, as much as he was able ; as if baptized a second time with his own tears, and only concealing his right hand. But the Apostle pledging himself, and solemnly assuring him, that he had found pardon for him in his prayers at the hands of Christ, praying on his bended knees, and kissing his right hand as cleansed from all iniquity, conducted him back again to the church. Then supplicating with frequent prayers, contending with constant fastings, and softening down his mind with various consolatory declarations, he did not leave him, as it is said, until he had restored him to the church. Affording a powerful example of true repentance, and a great evidence of a regeneration, a trophy of a visible resurrection."

The other story is given on the authority of Jerome, and is to the effect that when St. John became too old to take much active part in the work of the church, or to speak for any length of time, he used to be carried into the Christian assembly. On such occasions he always repeated the same words, " Little children, love one another." On being asked why he always said this he replied, " Because it is the commandment of the Lord, and if this alone be done, it is sufficient."

These stories are fully consistent with the idea which the church at large has formed of the beloved apostle. A venerable figure, gracious and tender, he lives in the reverence of the Christian church as a model of Christian character, the ripe fruit of the sacred influence generated by the Son of Man on the lake shore of Galilee and the upper room at Jerusalem.

R. J. CAMPBELL.

ST. JOHN AND THE APOCALYPSE

ST. JOHN THE APOSTLE AND EVANGELIST. AFTER THE PAINTING IN THE PITTI GALLERY, FLORENCE, FROM
A PHOTOGRAPH BY BRAUN, CLÉMENT & CO., PARIS

Carlo Dolci, Florentine School
1616-1686

ST. JOHN AND THE APOCALYPSE

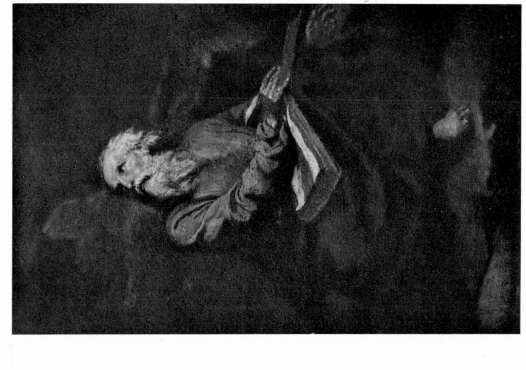

ST. JOHN AT PATMOS. AFTER THE ORIGINAL PAINTING, FROM A
PHOTOGRAPH BY W. A. MANSELL & CO., LONDON

J. L. E. Meissonier, Modern French School
1815-1891

ST. JOHN AT PATMOS. AFTER AN ORIGINAL MINIATURE IN A BOOK OF
HOURS AT CHANTILLY. THE PHOTOGRAPH BY GIRAUDON, PARIS

Jean Foucquet, French School
About 1415 towards 1480

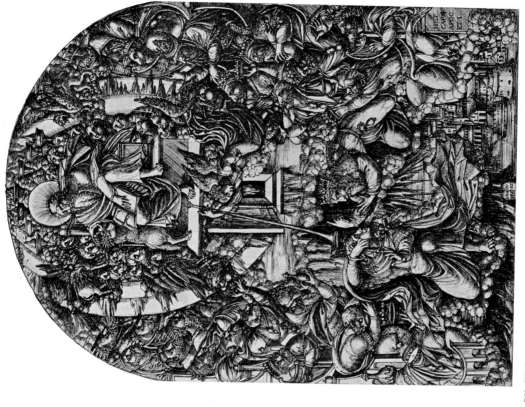

ST. JOHN AND THE APOCALYPSE

ST. JOHN'S VISION OF THE SEVEN GOLDEN CANDLESTICKS. "AND I TURNED TO SEE THE VOICE THAT SPAKE WITH ME. AND BEING TURNED, I SAW SEVEN GOLDEN CANDLESTICKS; AND IN THE MIDST OF THE SEVEN CANDLE-STICKS ONE LIKE UNTO THE SON OF MAN . . . AND OUT OF HIS MOUTH WENT A SHARP TWO-EDGED SWORD." (REVELATION I., 12-16)

Jean Duvet, French School
1485-1561

BY THE THRONE OF GOD IN HEAVEN THE LAMB THAT WAS SLAIN OPENS THE BOOK THAT IS SEALED WITH SEVEN SEALS. "AND ONE OF THE ELDERS SAITH UNTO ME, WEEP NOT: BEHOLD, THE LION OF THE TRIBE OF JUDA, THE ROOT OF DAVID, HATH PREVAILED TO OPEN THE BOOK, AND TO LOOSE THE SEVEN SEALS THEREOF." (REVELATION V., 5)

THE RIDER ON THE RED HORSE. "AND WHEN HE HAD OPENED THE SECOND SEAL, I HEARD THE SECOND BEAST SAY, COME AND SEE. AND THERE WENT OUT ANOTHER HORSE THAT WAS RED: AND POWER WAS GIVEN TO HIM THAT SAT THEREON TO TAKE PEACE FROM THE EARTH, AND THAT THEY SHOULD KILL ONE ANOTHER: AND THERE WAS GIVEN UNTO HIM A GREAT SWORD." (REVELATION VI., 3-4.) AFTER THE ORIGINAL PAINTING, FROM A PHOTOGRAPH BY F. HOLLYER, LONDON

G. F. Watts, O.M., R.A., Modern British School
1817-1904

THE RIDER ON THE WHITE HORSE. "AND I SAW, AND BEHOLD A WHITE HORSE: AND HE
THAT SAT ON HIM HAD A BOW; AND A CROWN WAS GIVEN UNTO HIM: AND HE WENT
FORTH CONQUERING, AND TO CONQUER." (REVELATION VI., 2.) AFTER THE ORIGINAL
PICTURE, FROM A PHOTOGRAPH BY F. HOLLYER

G. F. Watts, O.M., R.A., Modern British School
1817-1904

THE RIDER ON THE PALE HORSE. "AND I LOOKED, AND BEHOLD A PALE HORSE: AND HIS NAME THAT SAT ON HIM WAS DEATH . . . ." (REVELATION VI., 8.) AFTER THE ORIGINAL PAINTING, FROM A PHOTOGRAPH BY F. HOLLYER, LONDON

G. F. Watts, O.M., R.A., Modern British School
1817-1904

St. John and the Apocalypse

THE RIDER ON THE PALE HORSE: THE BARRICADE}
REPRODUCED FROM A WOODCUT LENT BY PROFESSOR A. LEGROS
Alfred Rethel, German School
1816-1859

St. John and the Apocalypse

The triumph of the rider on the pale horse. "And I looked, and behold a pale horse; and his name that sat on him was death, and hell followed with him. And power was given unto them over the fourth part of the earth, to kill with sword, and with hunger, and with death, and with the beasts of the earth." (Revelation VI., 8.) After the original etching

Professor A. Legros, Modern British School

St. John and the Apocalypse

THE FOUR HORSES AND THEIR RIDERS. "AND POWER WAS GIVEN UNTO THEM OVER THE FOURTH PART OF THE EARTH TO KILL WITH SWORD, AND WITH HUNGER, AND WITH DEATH, AND WITH THE BEASTS OF THE EARTH." (REVELATION VI., 8)

Albrecht Dürer, German School
1471-1528

St. John and the Apocalypse

THE TRIUMPH OF THE RIDER ON THE PALE HORSE: AFTER THE VICTORY. REPRODUCED BY KIND PERMISSION FROM THE ORIGINAL ETCHING

Professor A. Legros, Modern British School

ST. JOHN AND THE APOCALYPSE

THE OPENING OF THE SIXTH SEAL, "AND THE STARS OF HEAVEN FELL UNTO THE EARTH, EVEN AS A FIG
TREE CASTETH HER UNTIMELY FIGS, WHEN SHE IS SHAKEN OF A MIGHTY WIND." (REVELATION VI., 13)

Albrecht Dürer, German School
1471-1528

THE SAINTS AND THE ELECT WITH PALM BRANCHES. "AFTER THIS I BEHELD, AND, LO, A GREAT MULTI-
TUDE, WHICH NO MAN COULD NUMBER, OF ALL NATIONS, AND KINDREDS, AND PEOPLE, AND TONGUES,
STOOD BEFORE THE THRONE, AND BEFORE THE LAMB, CLOTHED WITH WHITE ROBES, AND PALMS IN THEIR
HANDS." (REVELATION VII., 9). FROM AN ORIGINAL WOODCUT

Albrecht Dürer, German School
1471-1528

THE OPENING OF THE SEVENTH SEAL. "AND I SAW
THE SEVEN ANGELS WHICH STOOD BEFORE GOD; AND
TO THEM WERE GIVEN SEVEN TRUMPETS." (REV. VIII., 2)

THE SOUNDING OF THE SIXTH TRUMPET. "AND THE
FOUR ANGELS WERE LOOSED . . . FOR TO SLAY THE
THIRD PART OF MEN. (REVELATION IX., 15)

THE ANGEL COMMANDING JOHN TO EAT THE LITTLE
BOOK "AND I TOOK THE LITTLE BOOK OUT OF THE
ANGEL'S HAND, AND ATE IT UP; AND IT WAS IN MY
MOUTH SWEET AS HONEY: AND AS SOON AS I HAD
EATEN IT, MY BELLY WAS BITTER." (REVELATION X., 10)

THE BEAST DESTROYETH THE TWO PROPHETS. "AND
WHEN THEY SHALL HAVE FINISHED THEIR TESTIMONY,
THE BEAST THAT ASCENDETH OUT OF THE BOTTOM-
LESS PIT SHALL MAKE WAR AGAINST THEM, AND SHALL
OVERCOME THEM, AND KILL THEM. (REVELATION XI., 7)

Jean Duvet, French School
1485-1561

THE GREAT RED DRAGON STANDING BEFORE THE WOMAN CLOTHED WITH THE SUN. (REVELATION XII., 1-4)
FROM AN ORIGINAL PRINT IN THE BRITISH MUSEUM

Jean Duvet, French School
1485-1561

St. John and the Apocalypse

ST. MICHAEL AND HIS ANGELS FIGHT WITH SATAN. "AND THERE WAS WAR IN HEAVEN: MICHAEL AND HIS ANGELS FOUGHT AGAINST THE DRAGON; AND THE DRAGON FOUGHT AND HIS ANGELS." (REVELATION XII., 7) DRESDEN GALLERY, THE PHOTOGRAPH BY W. A. MANSELL & CO.

Jacopo Robusti (il Tintoretto), Venetian School
1519-1594

ST. JOHN AND THE APOCALYPSE

SATAN CAST OUT INTO THE EARTH BY ST. MICHAEL. (REVELATION XII., 9). AFTER THE
ORIGINAL PAINTING IN THE LOUVRE, FROM A PHOTOGRAPH BY THE AUTOTYPE COMPANY,
74, NEW OXFORD STREET, LONDON

Raffaello Sanzio (Raphael of Urbino), Roman School
1483-1520

HIST · CAP · I · A · APOC ·

A BEAST WITH SEVEN HEADS AND TEN HORNS RISES OUT OF THE SEA, AND ALL THE WORLD WORSHIPS IT
(REVELATION XIII., 1-4)

Jean Duvet, French School
1485-1561

ST. JOHN AND THE APOCALYPSE

THE ADORATION OF THE REDEEMING LAMB. (REVELATION XIV., 1-5.) AFTER THE FAMOUS RETABLE IN THE CHURCH OF ST. BAVON AT GHENT, FROM A PHOTOGRAPH BY W. A. MANSELL & CO.

Hubert Van Eyck and Jan Van Eyck, Flemish School
1366(?)-1426   1390(?)-1440

THE SEVEN ANGELS WITH THE SEVEN GOLDEN VIALS FULL OF THE WRATH OF GOD. (REVELATION XV., 7). AFTER THE ORIGINAL CARTOON BY PERMISSION OF THE BERLIN PHOTOGRAPHIC CO., LONDON

Peter von Cornelius, German School
1783-1867

St. John and the Apocalypse

A WOMAN ARRAYED IN PURPLE AND SCARLET, WITH A GOLDEN CUP IN HER HAND, SITTETH UPON A SCARLET COLOURED BEAST, WHICH IS GREAT BABYLON, THE MOTHER OF ALL ABOMINATIONS. (REVELATION XVII., 3-5)

Albrecht Dürer, German School
1471-1528

St. John and the Apocalypse

THE ANGEL THAT COMES DOWN FROM HEAVEN, BINDS SATAN FOR A
THOUSAND YEARS. (REVELATION XX., 1-2)

Jean Duvet, French School
1485-1561

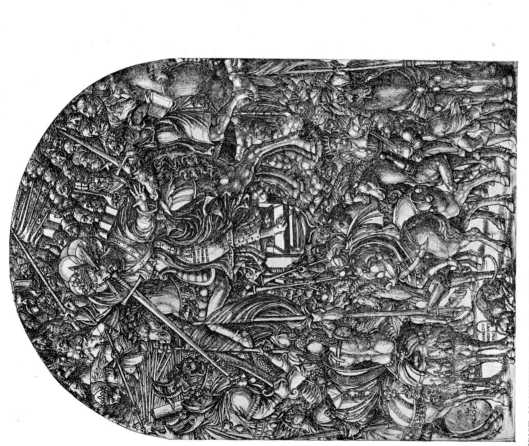

CHRIST MOUNTING ON THE WHITE HORSE FOLLOWED BY THE ARMIES OF
HEAVEN. (REVELATION XIX., 11-14)

St. John and the Apocalypse

The angel binding satan. "And I saw an angel, come down from heaven, having the key of the bottomless pit and a great chain in his hand. And he laid hold on the dragon, that old serpent, which is the devil, and satan, and bound him a thousand years . . ." (Revelation xx., 1-2)

Peter von Cornelius, German School
1783-1867

ST. JOHN AND THE APOCALYPSE

THE CALLING OF THE ELECT TO HEAVEN. (REVELATION XX., 4). A DETAIL OF THE FAMOUS FRESCO IN THE DUOMO, ORVIETO. FROM A PHOTOGRAPH BY ANDERSON, ROME

Luca Signorelli, Florentine School
1441-1523

THE FIRST RESURRECTION. (REVELATION XX., 4-5). AFTER AN ORIGINAL CARTOON IN THE MUSÉE DE LYON, FROM A
PHOTOGRAPH BY BRAUN, CLÉMENT & CO.

Paul Chenavard, Modern French School
Died in 1895

ST. JOHN AND THE APOCALYPSE

THE LAST JUDGMENT. AFTER THE STUPENDOUS WORK IN THE CAPPELLA SISTINA (A.D. 1541), FROM A PHOTO-
GRAPH BY ANDERSON

Michelangelo Buonarroti, Florentine School
1475-1564

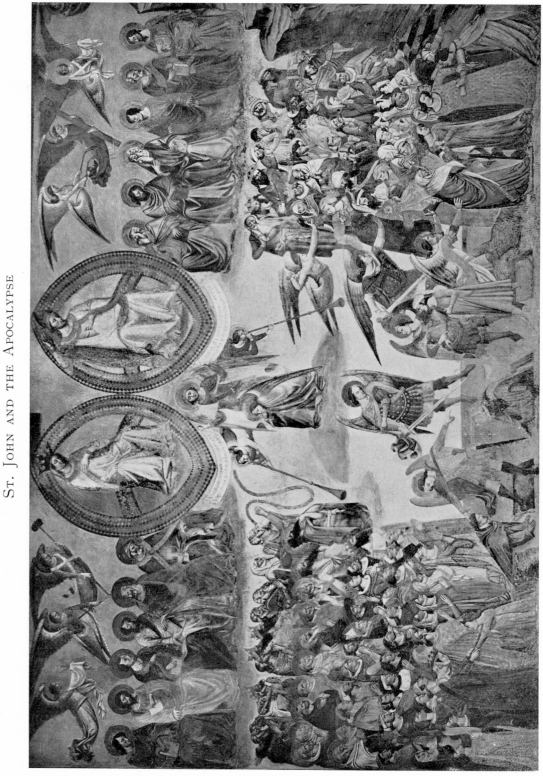

St. John and the Apocalypse

THE LAST JUDGMENT. AFTER THE ORIGINAL FRESCO IN THE CAMPO SANTO AT PISA, FROM A COPYRIGHT PHOTOGRAPH BY BRAUN, CLEMENT & CO., PARIS

Andrea di Cione, known as Orcagna, Florentine School
about 1308-1368

"AND THE SEA GAVE UP THE DEAD WHICH WERE IN IT." REVELATIONS XX. 13
AFTER THE ORIGINAL PAINTING IN THE TATE GALLERY, THE PHOTOGRAPH BY W. A. MANSELL

Lord Leighton, P.R.A., Modern British School
1830-1896

St. John and the Apocalypse

The Last Judgment. "And I saw the dead, small and great, stand before God; and the books were opened: and another book was opened, which is the book of life: and the dead were judged out of those things which were written in the books, according to their works." (Revelation xx., 12.)

John Martin, British School
1789-1854

ST. JOHN AND THE APOCALYPSE

THE DAY OF JUDGMENT   FROM AN ETCHING BY L. SCHIAVONETTI

William Blake, British School
1757-1827

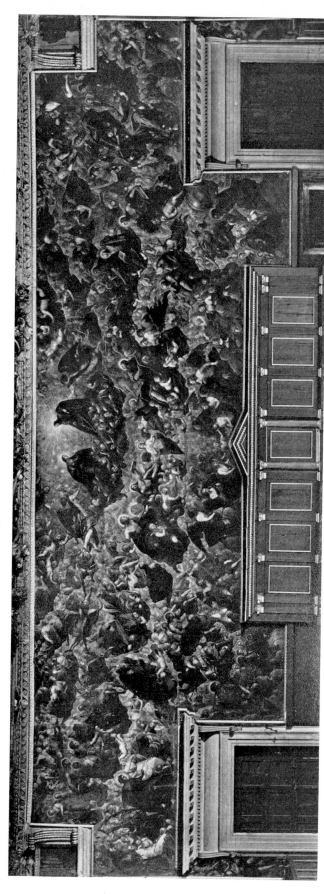

St. John and the Apocalypse

PARADISE—THE HEAVENLY JERUSALEM. "AND I SAW A NEW HEAVEN AND A NEW EARTH: FOR THE FIRST HEAVEN AND THE FIRST EARTH WERE PASSED AWAY . . ." (REVELATION XXI, 1). AFTER THE ORIGINAL WALL-PAINTING AT VENICE IN THE DUCAL PALACE, FROM A PHOTOGRAPH BY ANDERSON, ROME

Jacopo Robusti (il Tintoretto), Venetian School
1519-1594

St. John and the Apocalypse

THE PLAINS OF HEAVEN. "AND I SAW A NEW HEAVEN AND A NEW EARTH: FOR THE FIRST HEAVEN AND THE FIRST EARTH WERE PASSED AWAY; AND THERE WAS NO MORE SEA." (REVELATION XXI., 1)

John Martin, British School
1789-1854

DIES DOMINI. AFTER THE ORIGINAL DESIGN FROM A PHOTOGRAPH BY J. CASWALL SMITH, 309, OXFORD ST., LONDON

Sir Edward Burne-Jones, Bart., Modern British School
1833-1898

ST. JOHN AND THE APOCALYPSE

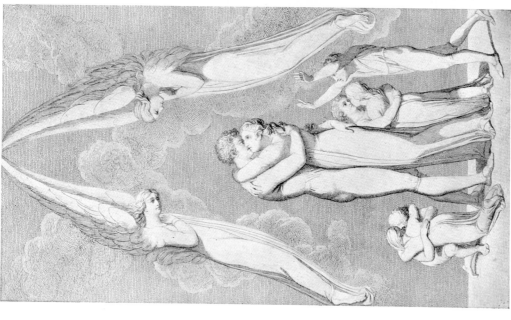

A FAMILY MEETING IN HEAVEN. FROM AN ETCHING BY L. SCHIAVONETTI

THE REUNION OF THE SOUL AND THE BODY. FROM AN ETCHING BY L. SCHIAVONETTI

William Blake, British School
1757-1827

St. John and the Apocalypse

AFTER THE LAST AND GENERAL RESURRECTION. "AND GOD SHALL WIPE AWAY ALL TEARS FROM THEIR EYES; AND THERE
SHALL BE NO MORE DEATH, NEITHER SORROW, NOR CRYING, NEITHER SHALL THERE BE ANY MORE PAIN; FOR THE FORMER
THINGS ARE PASSED AWAY." (REVELATION XXI. 4). AFTER THE ORIGINAL CARTOON, REPRODUCED BY PERMISSION OF THE
BERLIN PHOTOGRAPHIC CO., LONDON

Peter Von Cornelius, German School
1783-1867

St. John and the Apocalypse

THE ANGEL SHOWS ST. JOHN THE RIVER OF THE WATER OF LIFE AND THE TREE OF LIFE. (REVELATION XXII, 1-2). REPRODUCED FROM AN ORIGINAL PRINT IN THE BRITISH MUSEUM

Jean Duvet, French School
1485-1561

St. John and the Apocalypse

DRUSIANA RESTORED TO LIFE BY ST. JOHN THE EVANGELIST. THIS FRESCO AT FLORENCE, IN THE
CHIESA DI SANTA CROCE, IS A LEGENDARY INCIDENT. TRADITION RECORDS HOW ST. JOHN, AFTER
DWELLING FOR A YEAR AND A DAY IN THE ISLAND OF PATMOS, RETURNED TO HIS CHURCH AT
EPHESUS, AND MET BY THE CITY GATES THE FUNERAL OF DRUSIANA, WHOSE GOOD WORKS WERE A
SWEET MEMORY, AND WHOSE HOUSE HAD OFTEN BEEN A HOME TO JOHN

Giotto, Florentine School
1276-1335

ST. JOHN THE EVANGELIST, RISING FROM HIS TOMB TO HEAVEN, IS RECEIVED AND WELCOMED BY JESUS
CHRIST. AFTER THE LEGENDARY FRESCO AT FLORENCE, IN THE CHIESA DI SANTA CROCE, THE PHOTOGRAPH
BY ANDERSON

Giotto, Florentine School
1276-1335

LIST OF CONTRIBUTORS AND TABLE OF BLACK AND WHITE ILLUSTRATIONS

Angelico, Fra Giovanni, da Fiesole, called Beato Angelico, Florentine School. Born in 1387 at Vicchio, in Val Mugello. Died on the 18th of March, 1455, in Rome.

"ST. PETER IN THE ACT OF PREACHING WHILE ST. MARK TAKES DOWN HIS WORDS IN A BOOK" (p. 35). "ST. STEPHEN PREACHING TO THE PEOPLE," ACTS VI. 7-8 (p. 41). "ST. STEPHEN BEFORE THE HIGH PRIEST," ACTS VII., I. (p. 44). "THE MARTYRDOM OF ST. MARK" (p. 101.)

Barbieri, Giovanni Francesco, called il Guercino, Bolognese School. Born at Cento, near Bologna, in 1591; died in Bologna in 1666.

"ST. MATTHEW" (p. 26). "ST. JOHN WRITING HIS GOSPEL" (p. 28). "ST. MARK THE EVANGELIST" (p. 30). "ST. LUKE THE EVANGELIST" (p. 30).

Bartolommeo, Fra, Florentine School. Born in 1475 near the Porta di San Pier Gattolini, outside the walls of Florence; died on the 6th of October, 1517.

"ST. MARK" (p. 27).

Bellini, Gentile, Venetian School. Born about 1426-7; died 23rd of February, 1507.

"ST. MARK PREACHING AT ALEXANDRIA" (p. 100).

Beuckelaer or Beuclaer, Joachim, Flemish School. Born at Antwerp in 1530; died in 1570.

"ST. PETER AND ST. JOHN HEAL THE SICK" (p. 36).

Bida, Alexandre, Modern French School. See the List of Monochrome Plates.

Biermann, G., Modern German School. See the List of Rembrandt Photogravures.

Blake, William, British School. Born in 1757; died in 1827.

"THE DAY OF JUDGMENT" (p. 146). "THE REUNION OF THE SOUL AND THE BODY" (p. 149). "A FAMILY MEETING IN HEAVEN" (p. 149).

Buonarroti, Michelangelo, Florentine School. Born at the Castle of Caprese, near Arezzo, in 1475; died in Rome in 1564.

"CRUCIFIXION OF ST. PETER," (p. 96), "THE LAST JUDGMENT" (p. 143).

The Apostles in Art

Burne-Jones, Sir Edward, Bart., Modern British School. See the List of Monochrome Plates.

Cano, Alonso, Spanish School. Born at Grenada in 1601; and died there, the 5th of October, 1667.

"ST. PAUL THE APOSTLE" (p. 73).

Carpaccio, Vittore, Venetian School. Worked from 1490 to 1519.

"THE CONFIRMATION OF ST. STEPHEN BY ST. PETER" (p. 39). "ST. STEPHEN PREACH-ING," ACTS VI., 9-10 (p. 42). "ST. STEPHEN PREACHING AT JERUSALEM," ACTS VI., 10 (p. 43).

Cazes, Pierre Jacques, French School. Born in Paris in 1676; died in 1754.

"PETER HAVING RESTORED TABITHA TO LIFE PRESENTS HER TO THE SAINTS AND WIDOWS," ACTS IX., 41 (p. 53).

Cesari, Giuseppe, Neapolitan School. Born about 1560; died at Rome in 1640.

"THE MARTYRDOM OF ST. PAUL," (p. 97).

Champaigne, Philippe de, Flemish School. Born in Brussels in 1602; died in Paris in 1674.

"THE APOSTLE ST. PHILIP WITH HIS CROSS" (p. 99).

Chenavard, Paul, Modern French School. Died in 1895.

"THE CATACOMBS AND THE EARLIEST TIMES OF THE CHRISTIAN CHURCH IN ROME" (p. 103). "THE FIRST RESURRECTION" (p. 142).

Cima da Conegliano, Venetian School. Died about 1517.

"ST. PETER HEALS THE LAME MAN" (p. 36).

Cornelius, Peter von, German School. Born in 1783; died in 1867.

"THE SEVEN ANGELS WITH THE SEVEN GOLDEN VIALS FULL OF THE WRATH OF GOD" REVELATION XV., 7 (p. 137). "THE ANGEL BINDING SATAN" (p. 140). "AFTER THE LAST AND GENERAL RESURRECTION" (p. 150). SEE ALSO THE LIST OF MONOCHROME SPECIAL PLATES.

Danby, Francis, A.R.A., British School. See the List of Plates in Rembrandt Photogravure.

Dobson, William Charles Thomas, R.A. Modern British School. See the List of Monochrome Plates.

General Index

Dolci, Carlo, Florentine School. Born at Florence in 1616; died in 1686.

"THE TRADITIONAL MARTYRDOM OF ST. ANDREW ON THE TRANSVERSE CROSS" (p. 102). "ST. JOHN THE APOSTLE AND EVANGELIST" (p. 121).

Dürer, Albrecht, German School. Born at Nuremberg in 1471; and died there in 1528.

THE FOUR HORSES AND THEIR RIDERS," REVELATION VI., 8 (p.128). "THE OPENING OF THE SIXTH SEAL," REVELATION VI., 13 (p. 129). "THE SAINTS AND THE ELECT WITH PALM BRANCHES," REVELATION VII., 9 (p. 130). "A WOMAN ARRAYED IN PURPLE AND SCARLET, WITH A GOLDEN CUP IN HER HAND, SITTETH UPON A SCARLET COLOURED BEAST, WHICH IS GREAT BABYLON, THE MOTHER OF ALL ABOMINATIONS," REVELATION XVII., 3-5 (p. 138). SEE ALSO THE LIST OF MONOCHROME PLATES AND THE LIST OF PLATES IN REMBRANDT PHOTOGRAVURE.

Duvet, Jean, French School. Born in 1485; died in 1561.

"ST. JOHN'S VISION OF THE SEVEN GOLDEN CANDLESTICKS," REVELATION I., 12-16 (p. 123). "BY THE THRONE OF GOD IN HEAVEN THE LAMB THAT WAS SLAIN OPENS THE BOOK THAT IS SEALED WITH SEVEN SEALS" (p. 123). "THE OPENING OF THE SEVENTH SEAL," REVELATION VIII., 2 (p. 131). "THE SOUNDING OF THE SIXTH TRUMPET," REVELATION IX., 15 (p. 131). "THE ANGEL COMMANDING JOHN TO EAT THE LITTLE BOOK," REVELATION X., 10 (p. 131). "THE BEAST DESTROYETH THE TWO PROPHETS," REVELATION XI., 7 (p. 131). "THE GREAT RED DRAGON STANDING BEFORE THE WOMAN CLOTHED WITH THE SUN," REVELATION XII., 1-4 (p. 132). "A BEAST WITH SEVEN HEADS AND TEN HORNS RISES OUT OF THE SEA, AND ALL THE WORLD WORSHIPS IT," REVELATION XIII., 1-4 (p. 135). "CHRIST MOUNTING ON THE WHITE HORSE FOLLOWED BY THE ARMIES OF HEAVEN," REVELATION XIX., 11-14 (p. 139). "THE ANGEL BINDING SATAN FOR A THOUSAND YEARS," REVELATION XX., 1-2 (p. 139). "THE ANGEL SHOWS ST. JOHN THE RIVER OF THE WATER OF LIFE AND THE TREE OF LIFE," REVELATION XXII., 1-2 (p. 151).

Elsheimer, Adam, German School. Born at Frankfurt-am-Main in 1574; died in Rome, 1620.

"ST. PAUL, SHIPWRECKED ON THE ISLAND CALLED MELITA, IS UNHARMED BY THE VIPER HANGING FROM HIS HAND," ACTS XXVIII., 4-5 (p. 90).

Führich, Professor J., Austrian School. Born in 1800; died in 1876.

"ST. PETER AND ST. JOHN, BY PRAYER AND THE IMPOSITION OF HANDS, GIVE THE HOLY GHOST TO THE FIRST CONVERTS AT SAMARIA WHOM PHILIP THE DEACON HAS BAPTIZED," ACTS VIII., 15-17 (p. 48).

Foucquet, Jean, French School. Born at Tours, towards the year 1415; died about 1480. Court Painter to Louis XI.

"THE DESCENT OF THE HOLY GHOST ON THE DAY OF PENTECOST" (p. 25). "THE MARTYRDOM OF ST. STEPHEN" (p. 47). "THE MARTYRDOM OF ST. JAMES THE GREATER, SANCTUS JACOBUS MAJOR, THE SON OF ZEBEDEE AND THE BROTHER OF JOHN," ACTS XII., 1-2 (p. 54). "ST. JOHN AT PATMOS" (p. 122).

The Apostles in Art

Giotto di Bondone, Florentine School. Born in the year 1276, at Colle, at the Commune of Vespignano, a village of the Val Mugello, fourteen miles from Florence. Died in Florence, the 8th of January, 1337.

"DRUSIANA RESTORED TO LIFE BY ST. JOHN THE EVANGELIST" (p. 152). "ST. JOHN THE EVANGELIST, RISING FROM HIS TOMB TO HEAVEN, IS RECEIVED AND WELCOMED BY JESUS CHRIST" (p. 152).

Guercino, Bolognese School. See under Barbieri.

Guido, Bolognese School. See under Reni.

Hallward, Reginald, Modern British School.

"ST. PAUL ESCAPES FROM DAMASCUS," ACTS IX., 25 (p. 52). "ST. PAUL BEFORE FELIX (p. 88). "ONESIPHORUS VISITING ST. PAUL IN THE ROMAN PRISON," II. TIMOTHY I. 16-17 (p. 91).

Hübner, Rudolf Julius Benno, German School. Born in 1806; died in 1882.

"PHILIP THE DEACON AND THE MAN OF ETHIOPIA, A SERVANT OF GREAT AUTHORITY UNDER CANDACE QUEEN OF THE ETHIOPIANS," ACTS VIII.., 29-30 (p. 49).

Juanes, Juan de, known also as Vicente Joannes or Vicente Juan Macip, Spanish School. Born at Fuente de Higuera, in Valencia, 1523 ; died at Bocayrente, 1579.

"ST. STEPHEN ACCUSED OF BLASPHEMY BEFORE THE SANHEDRIN," ACTS VII., 56 57 (p. 45). "ST. STEPHEN IN THE SYNAGOGUE" (p. 46). "ST. STEPHEN LED TO HIS MARTYRDOM" (p. 46). "THE STONING OF ST. STEPHEN" (p. 46). "BURIAL OF ST. STEPHEN" (p. 46).

Kulmbach, Hans von, German School. Died in 1522.

"ST. PETER AND ST. PAUL LED TO PRISON IN ROME" (p. 93).

La Hyre, Laurent de, French School. Born in Paris in 1606 ; died there in 1656.

"THE SICK ARE BROUGHT FORTH INTO THE STREETS, AND LAID ON BEDS AND COUCHES THAT AT THE LEAST THE SHADOW OF PETER PASSING BY MAY OVERSHADOW SOME OF THEM," ACTS V., 15 (p. 40).

Legros, Professor Alphonse, Modern British School.

"THE TRIUMPH OF THE RIDER ON THE PALE HORSE" (p. 127). SEE ALSO THE LIST OF MONOCHROME PLATES.

Leighton, Lord, P.R.A., Modern British School. See the List of Plates in Rembrandt Photogravure.

Le Sueur, Eustache, French School. Born in 1617 ; died in 1655.

"ST. PAUL AT EPHESUS : THE BURNING OF THE MAGICAL BOOKS," ACTS XIX., 19 (p. 84).

General Index

Poussin, Nicolas, French School.   Born at Les Andelys in 1594; died in Rome, 1665.

"THE DEATH OF SAPPHIRA," ACTS V., 8-10 (p. 38).   "ST. PAUL AND ST. BARNABAS BEFORE SERGIUS PAULUS: ELYMAS STRUCK WITH BLINDNESS," ACTS XIII., 11 (p. 77). "THE SCOURGING OF PAUL AND SILAS," ACTS XVI., 22-23 (p. 79).   "THE ECSTATIC VISION OF ST. PAUL, IN WHICH HE WAS CAUGHT UP TO THE THIRD HEAVEN," II. CORINTHIANS XII., 2-4 (p. 85).

Raphael of Urbino.   See under Sanzio.

Rembrandt, Dutch School.   Born at Leyden, July 15, 1606; buried at Amsterdam, October 8, 1669.

"ST. MATTHEW" (p. 26).   "THE APOSTLE PAUL" (p. 74).   SEE ALSO THE LIST OF MONOCHROME PLATES.

Reni, Guido, Bolognese Schools.   Born at Calvenzano, near Bologna, in 1575; died at Bologna in 1642.

"ST. PETER" (p. 32).   "THE DISPUTE AT ANTIOCH BETWEEN ST. PETER AND ST. PAUL," (p. 82).   "THE MARTYRDOM OF ST. PETER" (p. 97).   SEE ALSO THE LIST OF MONOCHROME PLATES.

Restout, Jean, French School.   Born at Rouen in 1692; died in Paris in 1768.

"ANANIAS AND PAUL," ACTS IX., 17 (p. 51).

Rethel, Alfred, German School.   Born in 1816; died in 1859.

"THE RIDER ON THE PALE HORSE: THE BARRICADE" (p. 126).

Ribera, Josef de, Spanish School.   Born at Xativa near Valencia, 1588; died in Naples, 1656.

"ST. PETER" (p. 31).   "ST. BARTHOLOMEW" (p. 31).

Robusti, Jacopo, il Tintoretto, Venetian School.   Born at Venice in 1519; died May 31st, 1594.

"THE BEHEADING OF ST. PAUL," (p. 94).   "ST. MICHAEL AND HIS ANGELS FIGHT WITH SATAN" (p. 133).   "PARADISE—THE HEAVENLY JERUSALEM" (p. 147).

Rubens, Peter Paul, Flemish School.   Born at Siegen in 1577; died at Antwerp in 1640.

"ST. ANDREW THE APOSTLE" (p. 32).   "PAUL'S CONVERSION" (p. 50).

Sant, James, R.A., Modern British School. See the List of Plates in Rembrandt Photogravure.

General Index

Sanzio, Raffaello (Raphael of Urbino), Roman School. Born at Urbino in 1483 ; died in Rome, 1520

"PAUL'S CONVERSION" (p. 50). "ELYMAS THE SORCERER STRUCK WITH BLIND-NESS," ACTS XIII., 11 (p. 76). "ST. PAUL AND ST. BARNABAS AT LYSTRA," ACTS XIV., 13-14 (p. 78). "ST. PAUL IN PRISON AT PHILIPPI," ACTS XVI., 26 (p. 80). "ST. PAUL AT ATHENS," ACTS XVII., 32-34 (p. 83). "SATAN CAST OUT INTO THE EARTH BY ST. MICHAEL," (p. 134). SEE ALSO THE LIST OF MONOCHROME PLATES.

Sarto, Andrea del, Florentine School. Born in the Parish of Santa Maria Novella, Florence, the 16th of July, 1486, the son of a tailor named Agnolo. Died of the plague in Florence, the 22nd of January, 1531.

"ST. JAMES THE GREATER (SANCTUS JACOBUS MAJOR) WITH TWO CHILDREN" (p. 34).

Sassoferrato, Giovanni Battista Salvi, Roman School. Born at Sassoferrato in 1605 ; died in Rome in 1685.

"THE MADONNA IN PRAYER" (p. 29).

Schnorr, Julius, German School. Died in 1872.

"ST. PAUL AT MILETUS WITH THE ELDERS OF THE CHURCH OF EPHESUS," ACTS XX., 37-38 (p. 86)

Shields, Frederic, Modern British School.

"ST. PAUL THE AGED" (p. 75). SEE ALSO THE LIST OF MONOCHROME PLATES.

Signorelli, Luca, Florentine School. Born at Cortona in 1441 ; died in 1523.

"THE CALLING OF THE ELECT TO HEAVEN," REVELATION XX., 4 (p. 141).

Thornhill, Sir James, British School. Born at Weymouth in 1676 ; died in 1734.

"PAUL AND SILAS IN PRISON AT PHILIPPI," ACTS XVI., 29 (p. 81). "ST. PAUL BEFORE AGRIPPA II., AND HIS SISTER BERENICE," ACTS XXVI., 1 (p. 89).

Tintoretto. See under Robusti.

Titian, Tiziano Vecellio, Venetian School. Born at Pieve, chief town of Cadore, in 1477 ; died in Venice in 1576. See the List of Monochrome Plates.

Van Dyck, Sir Anthony, Flemish School. Born in Antwerp in 1599 ; died at Blackfriars, London, in 1641.

'ST. JUDE WITH HIS EMBLEM, THE HALBERD" (p. 28). "ST. MATTHIAS" (p. 33). "THE MARTYRDOM OF ST. PETER" (p. 97).

The Apostles in Art

Van Eyck, Hubert (1366 (?)—1426), and Jan van Eyck (about 1380 or 1390—1440), Flemish School.

"THE ADORATION OF THE REDEEMING LAMB" (p. 136).

Vannucci, Pietro. See under Perugino.

Vecellio, Tiziano. See under Titian.

Vinci, Leonardo da, Florentine School. Born in 1452 at Vinci, a fortified *borgo* on the western slopes of Monte Albano, between Pisa and Florence; died on the 2nd of May, 1519, at Cloux, near Amboise, France; buried on the 12th day of August, 1519, in the Cloister of the Royal Chapel of St. Florentin at Amboise.

"ST. JAMES THE LESS" (p. 33).

Watts, G. F., O.M., R.A., Modern British School. Born in London in 1817, of Welsh descent, like Sir Edward Burne-Jones; died in 1904. Elected A.R.A. in 1867, and R.A. in 1868.

"THE RIDER ON THE RED HORSE" (p. 124). "THE RIDER ON THE PALE HORSE" (p. 125). SEE ALSO THE LIST OF MONOCHROME PLATES

Werff, the Chevalier Adriaen van der, Dutch School. See the List of Monochrome Plates.

Wylie, Miss J., Modern British School.

"PAUL AND THE FAITHFUL AT TYRE," ACTS XXI., 5 (p. 87).

Zampieri, Domenico (il Domenichino), Bolognese School. Born at Bologna in 1581; died at Naples in 1641.

"ST. PETER IN PRISON IS AWAKENED BY THE ANGEL," (p. 56).

THE END